# THE AFRICAN ELEMENT IN GANDHI

# The African Element in Gandhi

ANIL NAURIYA

NATIONAL GANDHI MUSEUM

*in association with*

GYAN PUBLISHING HOUSE
New Delhi

The African Element in Gandhi

First Edition : 2006


The cover design depicts a tapestry by Sr. Gereon Custodis, C.P.S. originally published by Mariannhill Mission Press, South Africa. It is reproduced here with permission.

ISBN: 81-87458-13-5

Price : Rs. 290/-

*Published by:*
National Gandhi Museum
Rajghat, New Delhi-110002
Phones: 23311793, 23310168, 23328310
Fax: 91-011-23311793
E-mail: gandhimk@nda.vsnl.net.in
Web-site: www.gandhimuseum.org

*In association with:*
Gyan Publishing House
Publishers-Exporters
5, Ansari Road, Daryaganj,
New Delhi-110002
Phones: 23261060,23282060
Fax: 91-011-23282060
Email: gyanbook@vsnl.com
Web-site: http://www.gyanbooks.com

This book is a richly detailed account of the people and events surrounding Gandhi's experience in Africa and its aftermath. It provides an original narrative of how Gandhi's stance in relation to emancipatory struggles evolved over time, focussing especially on the period since the high noon of his South Africa days. The relationship between Gandhi, Africa and its leaders was mutually productive and symbiotic; a connection which has often been underanalysed.

Through extensive examples and a close reading of documents from the era, the author makes clear the significance of passive or civil resistance as a strategy and traces its contours over Gandhi's lifetime. The resulting book opens up fertile new areas of research and presents us with a holistic picture of the continuing relevance of Gandhi for Africans and Africa for Gandhi.

ANIL NAURIYA is a New Delhi-based lawyer and writes on contemporary history and politics.

**NATIONAL GANDHI MUSEUM**

*in association with*

**GYAN PUBLISHING HOUSE**

**ISBN: 81-87458-13-5** **PRICE Rs. 290/-**

# CONTENTS

## FOREWORD

Many books have been written on Gandhi's twenty-one years in South Africa, the birth of Satyagraha and the transformation of Gandhi from a lawyer-servant of the Indian community to a Mahatma. But, unfortunately, there is not a single book on the interaction of Gandhi with the African people and their leaders, and on the lasting impact of his life and philosophy on South Africa.

Gandhi himself is largely responsible for this omission. He said little of his discussions with African leaders of his time. He wrote in *Harijan* (July 1, 1939): "I yield to no one in my regard for the Zulus, the Bantus and the other races of South Africa. I used to enjoy intimate relations with many of them. I had the privilege of often advising them." Who did he advise and what was his advice? We do not know from his writings. It may be that he was concerned that the racist rulers would use any publicity to those discussions to allege a conspiracy against the racist order.

When Gandhi arrived in South Africa, the Africans had been defeated and virtually enslaved. Indian indentured labour had been treated as semi-slaves. The authorities had begun to break the promises made to them about land and freedom after indenture, and to harass the free Indians in order to force all but the workers under contract to leave.

The Europeans, and even many educated and Christian Africans, treated the Zulu masses as barbaric and uncivilized, calling them *kaffirs*. Little was known of the culture and civilization of the Africans. In countering arguments of the whites that Indians were uncivilized like the Africans and hence not entitled to civic rights, some of the early memoranda by Gandhi contain statements reflecting the current prejudices.

But as he came to know the Africans, he overcame the initial prejudices and developed great love and respect for the Africans. In 1908 he spoke of his vision of a South African nation in which "all the different races commingle and produce a civilization that perhaps the world has not yet seen".

His experiences in South Africa - his awareness of the savagery of the Anglo-Boer War, the heroism of the Boer women and the brutality of the white settlers in Natal during the Bambata rebellion against a poll tax - may well have inspired him to discover *satyagraha* as much as any books he had read. In turn, African leaders were inspired by the *satyagraha* in South Africa and the campaigns of civil disobedience in India led by Gandhi.

In 1946-48, when Gandhi was deeply distressed by the communal riots in India, as if his life's work had been in vain, the Indian community in South Africa was engaged in a great passive resistance campaign, with the support and solidarity of the African and Coloured people. He was encouraged that the spirit of *satyagraha* survived in the land of its birth, and guided the leaders of the resistance, Dr. Yusuf Dadoo and Dr. G. M. Naicker. When white hooligans brutally attacked non-violent resisters, including women, he declared: "I would not shed a single tear if all the *satyagrahis* in South Africa were wiped out. Thereby they will not only bring deliverance to themselves but point the way to the Negroes and vindicate the honour of India".

Leaders of the African National Congress were impressed by the sacrifices and the organizational ability of the Indians. In 1952, the ANC, in cooperation with the South African Indian Congress, launched the "Campaign of Defiance against Unjust Laws". Within a few years, the African-Americans, under the leadership of Dr. Martin Luther King, Jr., began mass non-violent resistance against racism in the United States. These great movements, which drew inspiration from Gandhi, shattered the myth that Africans were incapable of non-violent resistance. Active non-violence spread around the globe in colonial revolutions and the peace movements.

Mandela became a mass leader in 1952 as Volunteer-in-Chief of the Defiance Campaign, with Moulvi I.A. Cachalia, son of a close associate of Gandhi, as his deputy. The South African liberation movement since then has been honoured by Nobel Peace Prizes to three African leaders – Chief Albert Luthuli, Bishop Desmond Tutu and Nelson Mandela. That provides a fitting reply to those who criticized Gandhi for not venturing to lead the Africans but encouraging them to develop their own leadership.

I believe that Gandhi had an impact not only on the oppressed people of South Africa but also on the whites, and that the legacy of Gandhi was one of the factors which made possible the miracle of reconciliation which helped transform South Africa in the 1990s from a racist state to a non-racial democratic state.

Mr. Nauriya has made a thorough study of the letters, articles and speeches of Gandhi, and other available evidence, to produce this booklet on the evolution of his friendship and love for the African majority in South Africa. It is a valuable contribution for understanding Gandhi.

E. S. Reddy

New York,
November 2005

# PREFACE

Mohandas Karamchand Gandhi went to South Africa in 1893, as a young barrister on a short-term assignment. Within a few days he experienced a series of racial humiliations, including the well-known incident when he was thrown out of the first class train compartment at the Pietermaritzburg railway station on account of the colour of his skin.

Gandhiji remained in South Africa for 21 years. When he left it finally in 1914, he was already known for his philosophy and practice of nonviolent resistance to racial injustice, oppression and exploitation. This came to be described variously as passive resistance, civil resistance, civil disobedience or Satyagraha. In South Africa Gandhiji evolved and matured from an upper class Indian professional to a political mass leader of Indians cutting across classes in their struggle against racial discrimination. **In tandem with this evolution, he also came to envision, by the time of his Johannesburg speech on May 18, 1908, a multi-racial polity and society in South Africa.**

Gandhiji's role as a pathfinder in relation to African struggles was combined with an emphasis on non-violence. Although there were variations of technique and method over time and space, the "name of Gandhi has had repercussions" across Africa, to adopt a comment by George Bennett in his essay on "East and Central Africa" [in Peter Judd, (ed.) *African Independence*, Dell Publishing Co, New York, 1963, p. 402]. That Gandhiji's philosophy and half-a-century long nonviolent and mass-based struggles against racial discrimination in South Africa and against colonial rule in India acted as an inspiration in South Africa and elsewhere in Africa is indicated also by the history of the collapse of colonial rule in various countries in Africa after India attained freedom. African leaders like Nelson Mandela, Kwame Nkrumah, Albert Luthuli, Desmond

Tutu, Julius Nyerere, Kenneth Kaunda, among others, have in some form or another, acknowledged Gandhiji as an inspiration. Even a leader like Joshua Nkomo of Zimbabwe, who found Gandhiji's methods "not appropriate" to the "special national situation" in his country, nevertheless observes that Gandhiji's movements were "an inspiration to us, showing that independence need not remain a dream". [Nkomo (Joshua), *The Story of My Life*, Methuen, London, 1984, p. 73].

As one writer has put it: "Of all the Asian independence movements, the Indian movement has undoubtedly stirred the imagination of African nationalists the most. And it is not difficult to see why. First, there was the personality of Mahatma Gandhi. The message cabled by the National Council of Nigeria and the Cameroons (NCNC) on his death expressed the sentiments of all African nationalists, for whom Gandhi was the 'bearer of the torch of liberty of oppressed peoples' and whose life had been 'an inspiration to colonials everywhere'." [George H T Kimble, *Tropical Africa*, Volume 2: Society & Polity, The Twentieth Century Fund, New York, 1960, p. 285]

Gandhiji's struggle and method inspired and interested African-Americans as well. This became evident as articles relating to him and his activities began to appear in African-American journals at least as early as 1919. Hubert Harrison and Dr W E B DuBois were among the prominent African-American intellectuals who began to write and speak about him at this time. Later Gandhiji's method became a model for the African-American struggle under the leadership of Martin Luther King, Jr., as is well known.

Shri Anil Nauriya, a lawyer practising at the Supreme Court of India, has worked on India's freedom movement. He has also lectured in South Africa on the subject of this essay. The study was undertaken bearing in mind the growing need, with the passage of time, for an understanding of the abiding relationship that Gandhiji came to develop with Africans and their struggle for liberation and how he both contributed to, and learnt from, these struggles and experiences. The study is focussed on, but not confined to, South Africa. It provides also a sense of Gandhiji's live interface with the rest of Africa and the struggles of African-Americans. In conducting the study, Shri Nauriya has sought also to bring together a significant body of material which, though available, seems insufficiently utilized in current scholarship.

The study is a step toward filling a gap in the literature on Gandhiji. It also points the way for further work in this direction. The publication will be especially welcome at this time as it was precisely a century ago that Gandhiji propounded the ideology and technique of Satyagraha with the resolution on the subject being passed before a gathering of Indians in Johannesburg in the Transvaal, South Africa on September 11, 1906. He stressed the need for resistance of the so-called Asiatic Ordinance, or the "Black Act" as it came to be known upon its enactment by the Transvaal legislature, and insisted on a readiness to suffer the consequences of defiance, which could mean prison or worse.

This Museum is grateful to Shri Anil Nauriya for this painstaking and meticulously written thesis on the evolution of Gandhiji.

The Museum is obliged also to Shri E S Reddy for his Foreword. Mr Reddy, has been Assistant Secretary General of the United Nations, and was Director of the UN's Centre against Apartheid for a period of more than 20 years. A close friend of many leading figures in African liberation struggles, few are more familiar than he with the history of the South African struggle against racialism and colonialism. In addition, his has been a life-long pursuit of collection of historical records and information on the subject.

Dr. Y. P. Anand<br>
Director<br>
National Gandhi Museum,<br>
Rajghat, New Delhi- 110002

# I

## An Overview

*(i) "The Indians do not regret that capable Natives can exercise the franchise. They would regret it if it were otherwise. They, however, assert that they too, if capable, should have the right." Gandhi in The Times of Natal, October 26, 1894 (The Collected Works of Mahatma Gandhi, (CW) Volume 1, p. 166).*

*(ii) "They can use the powerful argument that they are the children of the soil... We can petition the Secretary of State for India, whereas they cannot. They belong largely to the Christian community and can therefore avail themselves of the help of their priests. Such help is not available to us." (Gandhi in Indian Opinion, March 24, 1906, CW, Vol 5, p. 243)*

*(iii) " We hear nowadays a great deal of the segregation policy, as if*

*it were possible to put people in water-tight compartments." (Gandhi, speaking in Johannesburg, May 18, 1908, CW, Vol 8, p. 243)*

*(iv) "If we look into the future, is it not a heritage we have to leave to posterity, that all the different races commingle and produce a civilisation that perhaps the world has not yet seen?" (Gandhi in his Johannesburg Speech, May 18, 1908, CW, Vol 8, p. 246)*

*(v) "Indians have too much in common with the Africans to think of isolating themselves from them. They cannot exist in South Africa for any length of time without the active sympathy and friendship of the Africans. I am not aware of the general body of the Indians having ever adopted an air of superiority towards their African brethren, and it would be a tragedy if any such movement were to gain ground among the Indian settlers of South Africa.... And what is more, the South African whites are able to translate their contempt and prejudice against us into action whereas ours towards the South Africans can only react against ourselves." (Gandhi in Young India, April 5, 1928, CW, Vol 36, p. 190)*

*(vi) " England has got successful competitors in America, Japan, France, Germany. It has competitors in the handful of mills in India, and as there has been an awakening in India, even so there will be an awakening in South Africa with its vastly richer resources — natural, mineral and human. The mighty English look quite pigmies before the mighty races of Africa. They are noble savages after all, you will say. They are certainly noble, but no savages and in the course of a few years the Western nations may cease to find in Africa a dumping ground for their wares." (Gandhi, speaking at Oxford, October 24, 1931, CW, Vol 48, p.225)*

*(vii) "You, on the other hand, are the sons of the soil who are being robbed of your inheritance. You are bound to resist that. Yours is a far bigger issue." (Gandhi to Rev S.S. Tema, member of the African National Congress, January 1, 1939, CW, Vol 68, pp 272-273.)*

It is usual to record Gandhi's evolution in South Africa and his application of passive resistance or Satyagraha to achieve political objectives. Gandhi's campaigns in South Africa resulted in his being incarcerated at various times in the early twentieth century in Johannesburg, Pretoria, Dundee, Volksrust and Bloemfontein jails. In the end Indian women also participated in these campaigns and filled many prisons. Gandhi's wife Kasturba, along with other Indian women including Valiamma, was imprisoned in Pietermaritzburg jail.

This essay builds upon and incorporates material prepared for a lecture delivered by the author at the Indian Cultural Centre in Durban on June 29, 2004. It attempts to focus not so much on Gandhi's campaigns on behalf of Indians in Africa as to explore the interface between Gandhi and the African struggles. This includes Gandhi's positioning himself in empathy with the educational network then available to Young Africa, his choice of a settlement in Phoenix, next not only to the Inanda center of Isaiah Shembe and of the Inanda Seminary but also to the Ohlange institution established by John Dube who was praised by Gandhi in 1905 and who was in 1912 to be the first President-General of the African National Congress (then called the South African Native National Congress); Gandhi's contact with the Trappists of Mariannhill, who in 1891 had been described by the Umtata Herald as unique "educators for a people who still have to obtain their sustenance by means of agriculture and handwork"; and his support for John Tengo Jabavu's educational initiative at Lovedale.

These were criss-crossing currents: Dube is the author of a book on Shembe, another of Dube's books is published by Mariannhill, and Dube's journal is printed initially at the International Press set up by Madanjit Vyavaharik where *Indian Opinion* was also printed.

It is probably fair to say that such interactions along with the successively wider nature of the mass struggles led by Gandhi helped expand his own horizons. In a deeply striking way, Gandhi seems to furnish an instance of 'becoming the change that you wish to see'. The young lawyer, not yet 24, had been brought to South Africa by Indian merchant clients and initially shared some of the racial and class prejudices prevalent among those for whom he worked. He tended sometimes to use the term Kaffir, then current among both Europeans and Indians settled in South Africa, to refer to the bulk of the African population. As a subject of the British Empire, as Gandhi then saw himself, he sought non-discrimination by the European but resented the equation of the educated section of Indians with the 'raw native'. If, however, the young Gandhi shared any prejudices towards sections of the population, he outgrew these by around 1908, that is some six years before he left Africa.

E S Reddy has noted that contrary to certain attempts to suggest that Gandhi spoke only for Indian merchants, the fact is that those who followed him in passive resistance in the Transvaal a hundred years ago in 1907 and the thousands who went on strike in Natal in 1913 "were mostly working people from South India and Hindustanis".

As we see Gandhi outgrow class limitations, so too emerges his mature perspective on the future development of Africa; by 1908 we hear him, now in his late thirties, urge "that all the different races commingle and produce a civilisation that perhaps the world has not yet seen". And by 1909 it is Gandhi, still a couple of months short of 40, who commends Thoreau's *Civil Disobedience* to the Coloured Peoples' leader, Dr Abdurrahman. In the following year, Gandhi welcomes the election of the African leader, Rev Dr Walter Rubusana, (a future Vice President of the yet to be born South African Native National Congress, later to be known as the ANC) to the Cape Provincial Council.

In July 1911 Gandhi's journal, *Indian Opinion*, notes the activities of (Pixley) Seme towards the formation of the future ANC and in January 1912 welcomes the founding of the organisation in January 1912 with John Dube as President as "an awakening" (*Indian Opinion*, February 10, 1912). Later in 1912, Gandhi takes the visiting Indian leader Gopal Krishna Gokhale to visit John Dube at the Ohlange Institute.

In the following year, *Indian Opinion* welcomed and gave prominence to the African Women's struggle in Orange Free State and supported John Dube's criticism of the Natives Land Act.

Working among Indians in South Africa, Gandhi was aware of the wider African implications of his work, many of which had become visible before he left Africa in 1914.

Visiting England in 1931 he was to make it clear of those South African races who "are ground down under exploitation" that: "Our deliverance must mean their deliverance. But, if that cannot come about, I should have no interest in a partnership with Britain, even if it were of benefit to India." (*Young India*, November 19, 1931, *CW*, Vol 48, p. 261).

It is this Gandhi, with his mind opened in Africa, as it were, who goes on to lead the struggle in India and, in 1943, to reiterate to the British Government even from behind prison walls that he sought the freedom of India as "an earnest and promise" of similar freedom for "all other subject peoples in Asia and Africa", a statement to which the eminent Nigcrian leader, Dr Nnamdi Azikiwe was to direct the attention of a British audience some years later.

Growing in empathy with increased experience of South African developments, Gandhi explored scope for co-operation with Africans, although he was for many years cautious about possibilities of an actually amalgamated struggle. **But by 1946-47 he endorsed joint struggle as well, while continuing to emphasise non-violence.** (*CW*, Vol 83, p.353 and *CW*, Vol 87, p. 28).

Gandhi had become, both before and after his assassination in 1948, a source of inspiration in Africa, about which Nelson Mandela has written so eloquently. Various South African movements that followed in 1913, 1919, 1946-48 and 1952 often carried, in diverse ways and degrees, a Gandhi stamp.

There were to be debates within the African National Congress and in Africa as a whole on the subject of non-violent struggle which in some way paralleled similar debates that had taken place continually and particularly in 1934 in the Indian National Congress.

The freedom movements both in India and in Africa were to seek and to find their own answers to the question, but the fact of the debate ensured an element of deliberation which earned a measure of universal respect for freedom movements in both continents.

In a 1956 preface to his autobiography, Kwame Nkrumah wrote: "After months of studying Gandhi's policy, and watching the effect that it had, I began to see that, when backed by a strong political organisation it could be the solution to the colonial problem." (*The Autobiography of Kwame Nkrumah*, Thomas Nelson & Sons, Edinburgh, 1959, p. vi).

Inevitably, this influence and interaction of ideas extended not merely to such parts of Africa as were under British rule but also affected attitudes and struggles in other parts of that continent and in the rest of the world.

Dr W E B DuBois, the inspiration behind the Pan-African movement, referred to Gandhi in the context of resolving racial conflict especially in the American South:
"If we .... solve our antithesis; great Gandhi lives again. If we cannot civilise the South, or will not even try, we continue in contradiction and riddle." [W E B DuBois, *Will the Great Gandhi Live Again*?, *National Guardian*, February 11, 1957, in David Levering Lewis (ed.), *W E B DuBois: A Reader*, Henry Holt & Company, New York, 1995, p. 360 ].

He wrote that it may well be that " real human equality and brotherhood in the United States will come only under the leadership of another Gandhi." (W E B DuBois, *Gandhi and the American*

*Negroes, Gandhi Marg*, Bombay, July 1957, Vol 1, Number 3, p.177).

Around the same time as Nkrumah wrote his *Autobiography*, Dr Martin Luther King recorded the contribution of the Gandhian method of non-violent resistance towards building in the United States "one of the most potent weapons available to the Negro in his struggle for freedom." (Martin Luther King, Jr., *Stride Toward Freedom: The Montgomery Story*, Harper & Brothers, New York, 1958, p. 85).

In this essay an attempt has been made to examine Gandhi's wider African concerns, within and outside the South African context, and to see how this interaction influenced African struggles as well as Gandhi's own understanding and movements. While Gandhi is known to have inspired generations of African thinkers and leaders, and to have, in turn, been influenced by African struggles, this impact and interaction needs to be the subject of further study.

The present essay is a contribution to the Satyagraha Centenary being observed in 2006. While the first two sections seek to introduce the subject and to place it in its context, sections III to X of the essay run, mainly, along a timeline. The sections are merely for reading convenience and actually form a connected whole along with section XI, the Epilogue.

## II

### The Context: "Yours is a far bigger issue"

The generations in England, India and South Africa which were witness to Gandhi's struggles by and large understood the complexities of the circumstances under which he lived and worked in the three countries. To have such a "feel" for the times is what may be called a sense of history. It is part of the essential equipment of a historian who would understand the period. Some of Gandhi's earlier remarks regarding Blacks with whom he came into contact, could be seen as dismissive and disparaging regardless of what Gandhi's intention may have been. However, such remarks were, with extended experience, not made after 1908. There was a definite widening in Gandhi's outlook and growth in his understanding. It is that widening that is implicitly celebrated when Gandhi is celebrated.

A consideration of Gandhi's attitude towards the Boer War and the Zulu Rebellion also needs to be informed with the understanding that at this point Gandhi was working for rights within the framework of the British Empire. He felt that rights flowed from duties and as such he offered his nursing and medical assistance to the British. His attitude towards the Great Indian Revolt of 1857 was, at this time, quite similar. (*Indian Opinion*, July 9, 1903, *CW*, Vol 3, p. 357).

Another issue concerns the fact that Gandhi did not draw in Blacks into his movements.

The laws governing Blacks and Indians in South Africa were different. The provocations for protest were therefore often different. "Their struggles are of different types", Gandhi wrote. (*Indian Opinion*, July 27, 1907, *CW*, Vol 7, p. 125) As a random illustration he points out that the Cape Immigration Act caused hardship to the Indian community but had little effect on Africans. (*Idem*) Of the Africans, he said, "as South Africa is their mother country, they have a better right here than we have" (*Idem*). Each – the Africans and the Indians – have, in the context of their respective struggles, "some advantages over the other" (*Idem*). In the Cape there was a limited franchise for Indians and Africans. Gandhi advised: "If the natives and the Indians of the Cape realize the value of the vote, they can still bring about many changes", even though it was "not absolutely necessary" that African and Asian votes "should always be cast on the same side". (*Idem*).

Although their struggles would not always converge, nevertheless, Gandhi had given thought to the question of mixing the African struggle with the Indian. At the time he considered the matter – in the infant years of the 20th Century – the issue was posed in the following terms: Indians in South Africa had started a struggle and had to decide whether to involve Africans in their travails. Gandhi decided against doing so not out of a lack of sympathy for the Africans but precisely because of his concern for them. Indians had another country – India – to fall back to. Africans did not. The consequences of the struggle could be different for Africans and Indians. As the one leading the struggle, he had to consider these. Most Indians at this time were indentured labourers, a system of slavery in another form as Gandhi described it (*Indian Opinion*, October 3, 1908, *CW*, Vol 9, pp. 82-83) or a "state of semi-slavery", as he called it on another occasion (Samalochak, December 1915, *CW*, Vol 13, p. 146).

This system was finally abolished later as a result of public pressure generated largely by the Gandhi-led campaigns in South Africa and India. Agitation by Indians in South Africa could mean hardships, but the Colonialists had possible remedies for most of them: imprisonment or deportation to India or the first followed by the second. The deportation remedy did not exist for the Africans. If the Africans came into the struggle and violence was resorted to there could have been prolonged repression of which the Africans would have had to bear the main brunt. Gandhi had already witnessed the brutality with which the Zulu rebellion was suppressed. We saw later what happened in South Africa in roughly the second half of the twentieth century once the organised African struggle began. That experience appears to have vindicated Gandhi's early decision.

In 1936 Gandhi was asked by an African-American delegation to India: "Did the South African Negro take any part in your movement?" Gandhi replied: "No, I purposely did not invite them. It would have endangered their cause." (*CW*, Vol 62, p.199).

Reluctant at this stage to call for a common front, he told the Press on July 8, 1939: "Bantus can only damage and complicate their cause by mixing it up with the Indian" (*CW*, Vol 69, p. 408). He advised against a non-European front. However he added in the same article that his advice "should not deter the Indians from forming a non-European front if they are sure thereby of winning their freedom."

Earlier, speaking on January 1, 1939 to Rev SS Tema of the African National Congress, he had expressed his doubts about the advisability of a non-European Front. But, in Gandhi's view, even without a joint front, there could be co-operation. Reminding Tema that the African issue was "far bigger", Gandhi told him: "The Indians can co-operate with you in a number of ways. They can help you by always acting on the square towards you. They may not put themselves in opposition to your legitimate aspirations, or run you down as 'savages' while exalting themselves as 'cultured' people in order to secure concessions for themselves at your expense." (*Harijan*, February 18, 1939, *CW*, Vol 68, p. 273)

Though cautious at this time about an amalgamated struggle, Gandhi provided a neat formula for mutual understanding. He declared that if Indian rights conflicted with African "vital interests", he would "advise the forgoing of those rights" (*Harijan*, July 1, 1939, *CW*, Vol 69, p. 377).

He was in touch with Dr Yusuf Dadoo and Dr G M Naicker who sought in the 1940s to build a joint struggle of Indians, Africans, the Coloured People and the liberal-minded whites. This was with Gandhi's support. Dr Dadoo was a Marxist who in his student days in India at the Aligarh Muslim University had opposed sectarian (or "communal") politics. Like Dr Naicker, he admired Gandhi. (See E S Reddy, *Gandhiji's Vision of a Free South Africa*, Sanchar Publishing House, New Delhi, 1995, pp. 108-112).

With the changed situation in South Africa, where a new South Africa-born Indian generation had come to the fore, Gandhi endorsed a joint struggle. However he did maintain that it ought to be non-violent. (E S Reddy, *Ibid*., pp 55-61). A deputation from South Africa led by Sorabji Rustomji came to India in 1946 (*CW*, Vol 83, pp 352-354). It was protesting against racial legislation in South Africa. A member of the delegation asked Gandhi: "You have said we should associate with Zulus and Bantus. Does it not mean joining them in a common anti-white front? " Gandhi replied: "Yes, I have said that we should associate with the Zulus, Bantus, etc.... It will be good, if you can fire them with the spirit of non-violence". (*CW*, Vol 83, p 353) Gandhi remarked of the deputationists' cause on May 27, 1946: "The cause is the cause of the honour of India and through her of all the exploited coloured races of the earth, whether they be brown, yellow or black. It is worth all the suffering of which they are capable". (*CW*, Vol 84, p. 215).

Gandhi's article in the *Harijan* of September 22, 1946 sums up his attitude:

"News comes from Durban that a group of Indians has sprung up in South Africa who have lost faith in satyagraha. They cherish the dream that they can overthrow the rule of the White man there, only by joining forces with the Negroes, the coloured people, other Asiatics and European sympathizers and adopting violent means. The rumour, if there is any truth in it, is disturbing and a definite fly in the ointment. All, whether they believe in non-violence or not, should realise that Indians in South Africa gained world-wide esteem simply because in spite of being a handful, they showed infinite capacity for suffering and did not, through losing their patience, resort to sabotage and violence. They learnt the wholesome lesson that true well-being springs from suffering and that victory lies in unity. From my own experience, my firm advice to Indians in South Africa is that they should, on no account, be lured away into throwing aside the matchless weapon of satyagraha.

This does not, however, imply that they are not to accept the help of the coloured people, Negroes and any other sympathizers or that they will not help them in their need, should occasion arise. The only condition is that satyagraha should be their one and only weapon." (*CW*, Vol 85, pp. 297-298).

In August 1946 tens of thousands of African mine workers had gone on strike for an increase in their miserable wages and working conditions. They were brutally suppressed and several were killed by the police. The Indian Passive Resistance Councils of Natal and Transvaal, in the midst of their own struggle, helped the Africans. Dr. Dadoo was charged with incitement of the strike, tried while he was already in prison for defying the Ghetto Act, but later acquitted. Some Whites, Africans, and Coloured People had also participated at this time in passive resistance in solidarity with the Indians and had also gone to prison . This unity is here being endorsed by Gandhi (see **Section X** below). The number was small and symbolic as the issue was Indian rights but it heralded a wider unity.

The same number of the journal *Harijan* ( September 22, 1946) carried a statement by Jawaharlal Nehru: "The issue raised in South Africa is something more than an Indian issue. It is an issue which affects all Asians and, of course, all Africans. Therefore, this co-operation is necessary between all those affected. But the co-operation can only be effective and succeed on the basis of peaceful methods and it would be folly to indulge in violence."

While in South Africa, Gandhi reached out to Africans like John Dube who was later to be the first President-General of the African National Congress. Dube who, like Gandhi, admired Booker T Washington, ran an industrial school, the Ohlange Institute, in Inanda near Phoenix. "There was frequent social contact between the inmates of the Phoenix settlement and the Ohlange Institute" (See E S Reddy, *Gandhiji's Vision of a Free South Africa*, op. cit. p.49). Reddy writes that John Dube's paper *Ilange lase Natal,* ("Sun of Natal"), an African weekly in English and Zulu, used to be printed in the *Indian Opinion* press until the Ohlange Institute acquired a press of its own. Gandhi commended Dube's work as he did that of Tengo Jabavu to set up a college for Africans. (See also *CW*, Vol 5, p. 55). There appear to have been some early African-American contacts as well. With Dube's education in America, African-Americans had a close association with Ohlange. According to one account, an African-American woman, Miss Blackburn, was Superintendent of the Students' hostel at Ohlange and she "often came to Phoenix". (Sushila Nayar, *Mahatma Gandhi: Satyagraha at Work, Volume IV, Navajivan Publishing House*, Ahmedabad, 1989, p. 714).

During his major struggles in South Africa and after his return to India in 1915 Gandhi remained conscious that when he worked for Indian rights or for Indian freedom back in India, it would be of benefit to other oppressed peoples. Gandhi said on July 12, 1944: "Today there is no hope for the Negroes, but Indian freedom will fill them with hope" (*CW*, Vol 77, p.351) . He knew that his struggles were based on and advanced the principle of racial equality regardless of who immediately suffered for that cause by direct participation in movements connected with it.

## III

### The Widening Horizon: " I witnessed some of the horrors...."

On the franchise question in Natal, soon after the founding of the Natal Indian Congress, Gandhi who had turned 25 years old a bare three weeks earlier, declared: "The Indians do not regret that capable Natives can exercise the franchise. They would regret it if it were otherwise. They, however, assert that they too, if capable, should have the right." (*The Times of Natal*, October 26, 1894, *CW*, Vol 1, p. 166).

Soon after Gandhi's arrival in South Africa, he came into contact with Trappists, a Catholic order of largely German Monks who had settled in South Africa. It was initially for their vegetarianism, about which he had read in England, that he sought them out in Mariannhill, near Pinetown, a village "16 miles by rail from Durban". He was pleasantly surprised by what he found and praised them for their good treatment of Africans: "They believe in no colour distinctions. These Natives are accorded the same treatment as the whites. They are mostly children. They get the same food as the brothers, and are dressed as well as they themselves are." (*The Vegetarian*, May 18, 1895, *CW*, Vol 1, p.226). Gandhi noted that the Trappists "love and respect, and are in turn loved and respected by, the Natives living in their neighbourhood who, as a rule, supply them with the converts." (*Idem*).

The Order at Mariannhill, was founded by Francis Pfanner. "Red Wendell", as the Abbot has been called with reference to the name given to him by his parents, was perhaps too radical not only for the Church of Rome but also for the Trappists themselves. Ultimately, on the Abbot's death in 1909, Mariannhill was constituted into a separate Order. Among those who may have been there when Gandhi visited Mariannhill for the first time in 1895 were the second Abbot (Abbot Amandus Schoelzig) and a young Polish woman, Mary Lassak who, according to the official history of Mariannhill, " took charge of the girls and taught them". The emphasis on handwork and the various workshops – "blacksmiths', tinsmiths', carpenters', shoemakers', tanners' ", the oil machine and the printing department – had impressed Gandhi as had the convent and the skills taught there. A photograph suggests that sandal-making was also among the various vocations taught, a skill Gandhi was later to introduce into his own settlement. He found the quarters for the African inmates (there were 1,200 Africans living on the Mission) somewhat stuffy and cramped but on the whole he came back satisfied that the Trappists believed in no colour distinctions.

Certain features of Mariannhill, including the dignity of labour and the African presence that Gandhi noticed there, were to be introduced also in the settlements which Gandhi established in South Africa.

In India on a brief visit in the following year, Gandhi received news from South Africa leading him to protest in print on learning that African and Indian boys were used as targets and shot in their faces by a picnic party of European children in Natal. (*The Times of India*, October 20, 1896, *CW*, Vol 2, p. 87).

On returning in January 1897, Gandhi found that he was now even more unwelcome than before and he was in fact assaulted and nearly lynched by European gangs in the course of anti-Indian demonstrations in Durban.

When the Boer War broke out two years later, Gandhi found that: "The Volunteers who have gone to the front to fight for the Queen's cause are mostly those who took the most prominent part in the now notorious anti-Indian demonstration of 1897 in Durban". [*The Times of India (Weekly edition)*, December 9, 1899, *CW*, Vol 3, p. 119]. He decided that as the Indians "were British subjects, and as such demanded rights, they ought to forget their domestic differences, and irrespective of their opinion on the justice of the war, render some service, no matter how humble, on the battlefield during the crisis, even if it were to act as bearers of the wounded in the Volunteer camp." (*Idem*). He thus served along with some other Indians as part of the Ambulance Corps.

In October 1901 Gandhi sailed for India, having promised to return within a year if required by the Indian community. At the end of the following year, in December 1902, he was back in Durban.

It is now that a new phase in his evolution starts, in which he begins to see himself as more than a mere passer-by in South Africa.

A few months after his return to South Africa, Gandhi criticised the Bloemfontein Municipal Ordinance of the Orange River Colony under which "Natives" and "Coloured persons" could be "removed like criminals or cattle from one place to another at the sweet will of the Corporation" (*Indian Opinion*, August 6, 1903, *CW*, Vol 3, p. 399).

The Johannesburg Town Council earned a sharp rebuke from Gandhi for the proposal that "every Native holding a cycle permit and riding a cycle within the municipal area, should wear on his left arm, in a conspicuous position, a numbered badge which shall be issued to him together with his permit". Gandhi referred to this as "persecution" and praised the minority in the Council who "did not hesitate to defend the Native against unnecessary and wanton indignity." (*Indian Opinion*, February 4, 1905, *CW*, Vol 4, p. 347).

A few months later Gandhi raises his voice again against the report of the Native Commission under which the Coloured community in the Transvaal, even if already enfranchised, would retain the franchise only in provincial elections but lose it "in the event of elections for a Federal Parliament" (*CW*, Vol 4, p. 351). He deplored this as "being much at one with the general attitude adopted by the white population of South Africa towards the non-white. In matters of Colour prejudice, it is, unfortunately, almost impossible to convince by logical argument. Where blind prejudice rules, justice goes by the board. We are afraid that the Coloured community of the Transvaal will have to wait long before they succeed in securing the recognition of what we conceive to be their just rights. We trust that they will continue to protest against ill-considered treatment and to urge the inherent justice of their demands." (*Indian Opinion*, February 11, 1905, *CW*, Vol 4, p. 351). Gandhi declared: "We can only say that the Coloured community has our fullest sympathy in its endeavour to escape from political oblivion." (*Idem*)

In 1905 there was a move in the Transvaal to deprive and restrict African rights in land. Gandhi protested strongly against such a measure (*Indian Opinion*, August 12, 1905, *CW*, Vol 5, pp 39-40). He records that before the Boer War Africans had at least been free to own land in the Transvaal. In his writings he repeatedly points out that one of the justifications offered for the Boer War had been the treatment meted out to the Coloured races by the Dutch. It had therefore been presented as a "war of emancipation" (*Ibid.*, p. 39). Yet, Gandhi cites statements in support of the view that "the treatment the Coloured races have been receiving in the Transvaal since British occupation is worse than before." (*Idem*)

He puts Lord Selborne, the Governor of the Transvaal, on test by holding the administrator to his assertion that: "If in any respect the British administration is unjust to the Native, civilised or uncivilised, it is a blot and a stain on our administration, and one which I feel personally as an implication of disgrace." (*Indian Opinion*, August 12, 1905, *CW*, Vol 5, pp 39-40). Adds Gandhi: "May His Excellency have sufficient courage and strength to initiate the policy he has thus boldly enunciated!". (*Ibid.*, p. 40).

A few weeks later Gandhi quoted appreciatively a "very impressive" speech by John Dube in Natal. The Natal-born Dube, who was later to be the first President of the African National Congress, was a couple of years younger to Gandhi. In the course of what Gandhi described as an "eloquent speech", Dube argued that for the Africans "there was no country other than South Africa; and to deprive them of their rights over lands, etc., was like banishing them from their home." (*Indian Opinion*, September 2, 1905, *CW*, Vol 5, p. 55). Gandhi hailed Dube as an African "of whom one should know" (*Idem*). He referred appreciatively to Dube who "imparts education to his brethren, teaching them various trades and crafts and preparing them for the battle of life." (*Idem*). Gandhi remained impressed with and close to Dube.

An event that took place seven years later may be mentioned at this point. When the South African Native National Congress (later renamed African National Congress) was formed in January 1912 it was Dube who was chosen its first President-General. The formation of the great African party was hailed by Gandhi's *Indian Opinion* as an "awakening" (*Indian Opinion*, February 10, 1912). And in November 1912 took place the historic meeting, which is referred to below, between Gandhi, John Dube, and the Indian statesman Gopal Krishna Gokhale who was then visiting South Africa.

**Nelson Mandela was to observe more than 80 years later: "M.K Gandhi and John Dube, first President of the African National Congress were neighbours in Inanda, and each influenced the other, for both men established, at about the same time, two monuments to human development within a stone's throw of each other, the Ohlange Institute and the Phoenix Settlement. Both institutions suffer today the trauma of the violence that has overtaken that region; hopefully, both will rise again, phoenix-like, to lead us to undreamed heights."[*Nelson Mandela, Gandhi The Prisoner: A Comparison*, in B. R Nanda (ed.), *Mahatma Gandhi : 125 Years, Indian Council of Cultural Relations*, New Delhi, 1995, p. 8].**

Gandhi praised the efforts of the African educationist, John Tengo Jabavu, Editor of *Imvo Zabantsundu* ("Native Opinion"), to establish "an Inter-State Native College with the present Lovedale Institute as its nucleus." (*Indian Opinion*, March 17, 1906, *CW*, Vol 5, pp. 234). Of the plans for this now famous institution at Fort Hare, Gandhi wrote:

"It is proposed to develop the work to be undertaken by the new College on the same lines of industrial training" as at the Tuskegee Institute started by Booker T. Washington in America, and concluded: "All this can do nothing but good, and it is not to be wondered at that an awakening people, like the great Native races of South Africa, are moved by something that has been described as being very much akin to religious fervour. To them undoubtedly the work must be sanctified and hallowed, for it opens up a means to advancement of thought and gives a great impetus to spiritual development." (*Ibid*, pp 234-235).

In the same article Gandhi cited this as an example worthy of emulation by the Indian community. Incidentally, *Imvo Zabantsundu* which Jabavu edited was the first Bantu political paper. Jabavu, ten years Gandhi's senior, and the first African in the country to matriculate, is later understood to have also developed a Quaker connection.

Sometimes, as Gandhi pointed out, in spite of some common grievances the particular claims of the various communities had to be urged from different points of view. In spite of this "wise policy", Gandhi felt that "each can give strength to the other in urging their common rights." (*CW*, Vol 5, pp. 242). Gandhi wrote in the *Indian Opinion* of March 24, 1906 that " though the hardships suffered by those people and the Indians are almost of the same kind, the remedies are not identical. It is therefore proper that the two should fight out their cases, each in their own appropriate way." He praised a petition prepared by Coloured People in support of their rights in the Transvaal and Orange River Colony and welcomed their move to send Dr Abdurrahman to England to canvas support. (*CW*, Vol 5, pp. 243-4). *

In April 1906 Africans in Natal had revolted against the poll tax. Two policemen were killed in the revolt. In response some Africans "were prosecuted under the martial law, and twelve of them were condemned to death and blown up at the mouth of a cannon". (*Indian Opinion*, April 7, 1906, *CW*, Vol 5, p. 266). Gandhi's wry comment was " Twelve lives have been taken for two." (*Ibid.*, p. 267). He praised William Morcum who pointed out at a meeting in Maritzburg that as the two policemen had been killed before martial law was declared, the Africans "ought to have been tried by the Supreme Court.", that is, not under martial law. (*Idem*). Gandhi commended Morcum for holding his own even though "the whole meeting was against him, and though they hissed and hooted at him". (*Idem*).

It is around this time that Gandhi offered and raised a Stretcher-Bearer Corps in the Zulu Rebellion. This experience offered fresh perspectives to Gandhi. His position in this context may be compared with that of Charles Bradlaugh who served in the British Army in Ireland but came to sympathize with the Irish cause.

The same year, in September 1906, Indians in South Africa decided upon passive resistance against the Asiatic Registration Ordinance, which was directed against Asian residence in Transvaal. Gandhi went on a deputation to London and the ordinance was not approved by the British government. Soon after Gandhi returned from London,

* "Coloured" is a term which, apart from its wider meaning, was sometimes used in a special South African sense meaning a miscellaneous category comprising mainly people who were neither European nor indigenous African, but generally of mixed origin, and living largely in the Cape Province though present in other areas as well. The category included also Cape Malays or Cape Muslims usually descended from people brought in as slaves from India and South-East Asia. When the Indian immigrants started arriving in South Africa they were treated as yet another racial category and the laws applicable were different. Generally, the Coloured people were less discriminated against than the Indian. In the Cape the Coloured people had the franchise. Dr Abdurrahman, a well-known doctor in the Cape, himself of Indian extraction, was elected to the City and Provincial Councils and provided leadership to the Coloured people and espoused the unity of all the non-white people. A friend of Gandhi from his South Africa days, Dr Abdurrahman came to India at the head of a delegation in 1925.

Britain granted self-government to the Transvaal. The Transvaal Asiatic Registration Act, 1907 was then enacted. The Indian defiance and jail-going campaign against this measure started in the second half of 1907. Gandhi was arrested in December 1907.

The satyagraha lasted for several years and more than 2,000 people in the small Indian community courted imprisonment, some more than once.

As Edward Roux describes the events: "Gandhi and other satyagrahis were arrested and sentenced to imprisonment with hard labour. The gaols were soon full of them. The captive Gandhi was marched through the street, handcuffed and in prison clothes." (Edward Roux, *Time Longer Than Rope: A History of the Black Man's Struggle for Freedom in South Africa*, The University of Wisconsin Press, Madison, 1964, p. 105).

Reflecting on the 1906 events some 30 months after, and in implicit recognition of the legitimacy of their cause, Gandhi was soon to recommend passive resistance to the Africans. In an interview to *The Natal Mercury* Gandhi said, referring to fears that the Asian passive resisters could lead to a similar movement among Africans: "...if the natives were to adopt our methods, and replace physical violence by passive resistance, it would be a positive gain to South Africa. Passive resisters, when they are in the wrong, do mischief only to themselves. When they are in the right, they succeed in spite of any odds. It is not difficult to see in Natal, that, if Bambata, instead of murdering Inspector Hunt, had simply taken up passive resistance, because he felt that the imposition of the poll-tax was unjustifiable, much bloodshed would have been avoided...." (*The Natal Mercury*, January 6, 1909, *CW*, Vol 9, p.127).

The caveat against killing foreshadowed the Gandhian position in both the African struggle and in the struggle yet to come in India under his leadership.

Of the experiences he had at this time, Gandhi was to write later in *Satyagraha in South Africa*: "We found that the wounded Zulus would have been left uncared for, if we had not attended to them. No European would help to dress their wounds. Dr Savage, who was in charge of the ambulance, was himself a very humane person. It was no part of our duty to nurse the wounded after we had taken them to hospital. But we had joined the war with a desire to do all we could, no matter whether it did or did not fall within the scope of our work. The good Doctor told us that he could not induce Europeans to nurse the Zulus, that it was beyond his power to compel them and that he would feel obliged if we undertook this mission of mercy. We were only too glad to do this. We had to cleanse the wounds of several Zulus which had not been attended to for as many as five or six days and were therefore stinking horribly. We liked the work. The Zulus could not talk to us, but from their gestures and expression of their eyes they seemed to feel as if God had sent us to their succour." (*CW*, Vol 29, pp. 82-83). More than two decades after the rebellion Gandhi was to recall to Rev. S S Tema, a member of the African National Congress: "I witnessed some of the horrors that were perpetrated on the Zulus during the Zulu Rebellion. Because one man, Bambatta, their chief, had refused to pay his tax, the whole race was made to suffer. I was in charge of an ambulance corps. I shall never forget the lacerated backs of Zulus who had received stripes and were brought to us for nursing because no white nurse was prepared to look after them. And yet those who perpetrated all those cruelties called themselves Christians. They were 'educated', better dressed than the Zulus, but not their moral superiors." (January 1, 1939, *CW*, Vol 68, pp 273-274).

Gandhi saw and condemned the racial discrimination built into the legal systems prevailing in South Africa and the manner in which it operated against the Africans. In 1907 an African, Mtonga, who had been assaulted by some persons was himself found guilty by a jury. In his article entitled *Juries On Trial*, Gandhi wrote of the "abortion of justice" in this case, saying that Natal was no exception and that: "We believe that what happened in Natal is likely to happen, under similar circumstances, in any part of South Africa, or in any country conditioned as South Africa is." (*Indian Opinion*, June 1, 1907, *CW*, Vol 7, p. 1). He criticised the prevalent jury system: "In a place like South Africa, where there is no leisured class and where people of all nationalities congregate, the jury system is about the worst that could be devised in connection with the administration of justice. The inherent condition of success of trial by jury is that the accused is tried by his equals. It is an insult to man's intelligence to contend that there is any such trial in South Africa, when the question is as between whites and blacks." (*Ibid.*, p. 1).

Natal laws and regulations were sharply criticised by Gandhi for their racist content. For instance, about the jail regulations in the Natal, Gandhi wrote in a passage that deserves attentive reading: "From the Natal Government Gazette we gather that there are four classes of prisoners in Natal: white, Coloured, Indian and Kaffir. If any work is taken from the white or the Coloured prisoners, the Government will give them some reward. But the Indian or the Kaffir prisoners who do any work will get nothing. Moreover, the white and the Coloured prisoners are given a towel each, while the Indian and the Kaffir are not given even this as if they do not need it at all. The Government have, in this manner, created classes even among prisoners." (*Indian Opinion*, June 22, 1907, *CW*, Vol 7, p. 50).

Gandhi criticised a proposed Natal law under which Indians cultivating their own lands, who let them to Africans or other Indians, would be required to "pay on those lands double the tax that the Europeans pay" (*Indian Opinion*, July 6, 1907, *CW*, Vol 7, p. 74). His wry comment was: " Only the Europeans of South Africa are capable of such justice! But it has always been the way of the world to add humiliation to defeat." (*Idem*).

Of the two major political parties in the Cape — the (Dutch)

Afrikaner Bond and the (British) Progressive Party, Gandhi wrote: "We must admit that just now these two parties are in the condition of the pot calling the kettle black. They are both tarred with the same brush. Neither of them overflows with love for the blacks." (*Indian Opinion*, July 27, 1907, *CW*, Vol 7, p.125).

## IV

### Passive Resistance: "that all the different races commingle...."

In July 1907 Indian passive resistance began in the Transvaal against the Asiatic Registration Act.

A few weeks later, in an article entitled "Duty of Disobeying Laws", the American thinker and writer, Henry David Thoreau, is lauded by Gandhi for his role in the abolition of slavery. Gandhi wrote, drawing some characteristically contemporary activist conclusions: " He considered it a great sin that the Americans held many persons in the bonds of slavery. He did not rest content with this, but took all other necessary steps to put a stop to this trade. One of these steps consisted in not paying any taxes to the State in which the slave trade was being carried on. He was imprisoned when he stopped paying the taxes due from him. .... Historians say that the chief cause of the abolition of slavery in America was Thoreau's imprisonment and the publication by him ...". (*Indian Opinion*, September 7, 1907, *CW*, Vol 7, p. 217).

A week later, Thoreau was again quoted appreciatively by Gandhi and the following passage among others, from Thoreau, was reproduced in the Gujarati language: "I know this well that even if only one honest man in this State of Massachusetts refuses to pay taxes in order to oppose slavery, and is locked up in gaol therefor, it would be the abolition of slavery in America." (*Indian Opinion*,

September 14, 1907, *CW*, Vol 7, p. 230).

Gandhi paid warm tributes to Egypt's leader Mustafa Kamal Pasha who died in February 1908 in Cairo. (*Indian Opinion*, March 28, April 4, April 11, April 18, 1908, *CW*, Vol 8, pp. 166-167, pp. 174-176 pp 187-188, and p. 199). In the tribute published on April 4, 1908, Gandhi observed: "The occupation of the Sudan by the British and other similar events dealt a cruel blow to [the hopes of] Egyptian independence. But the Pasha remained undaunted" (*CW*, Vol 8, p. 175).

If Gandhi's movements were centred upon the Indians resident in South Africa, it was often alleged and feared, especially in Colonial circles, that his Passive Resistance and Satyagraha campaigns were giving ideas to the Africans or Kaffirs, the term then current. Gandhi had a cryptic response to the fear apparently shared by General Smuts: " General Smuts seems to fear the effect upon the Kaffirs of the success of a campaign of passive resistance. But how is it that laws were modified before? And, after all, is it not something to the good that Kaffirs should feel that, in any differences with the white race, there are milder arguments than the rifle and assegai?" (*Indian Opinion*, January 11, 1908, *CW*, Vol 8, p. 30). The fear of being swamped by passive resistance on a wider scale appears to have been a continual one among the ruling minority in South Africa. Gandhi was to refer to it again nearly four years later: " Others again declared that to yield to passive resistance was to court trouble with the Natives." (*Indian Opinion*, October 7, 1911, *CW*, Vol 11, p. 164).

Gandhi's moral indignation is discernible in his recording of the diverse facets of racial discrimination against Africans. Writing about his experiences in prison, Gandhi points out that "the vegetables served to the Kaffir prisoners consist mostly of the left-overs and peelings from the vegetables cooked for the whites." (*Indian Opinion*, March 21, 1908, *CW*, Vol 8, p. 152)

In April 1908 Gandhi warmly welcomed a Supreme Court judgement in favour of African settlement rights in Sophiatown. The Africans in question had been prosecuted by the Municipality for living outside a specified "Location." Gandhi wrote: "In the course of his judgement, Justice Wessels condemned the action of the municipality as tyrannical and stated that in a civilized country vested rights ought not to be disturbed. It is a happy thought that the Supreme Court has always dispensed perfect justice, as it has on this occasion." (*Indian Opinion*, April 4, 1908, *CW*, Vol 8, p. 177).

Within two weeks, the Johannesburg Town Council comes in for severe condemnation once again. Gandhi describes as "shameless', the Council's proposals for "the introduction of such measures as may secure the enforcement of regulations having the object of preventing Natives and Coloured persons from occupying premises in localities other than those approved by the Council; of prohibiting the acquisition by lease, purchase or otherwise by Natives and Coloured persons of property in localities other than such as may be approved by the Council; and the regulation of the use of streets and sidewalks by Natives." (*Indian Opinion*, April 18, 1908, *CW*, Vol 8, pp. 194-195).

The African races, Gandhi told a meeting of the Young Men's Christian Association in Johannesburg on May 18, 1908, "are entitled to justice, a fair field and no favour. Immediately you give that to them, you will find no difficulty." (*CW*, Vol 8, p. 245). South Africa, he declared, "would probably be a howling wilderness without the Africans" (*Ibid*., p. 242). He continued, expressly using the term "Coloured People" so as " to include the Coloured people proper - the Africans and the Asiatics", to declare that: "The majority of people in South Africa, the majority of people in most of the Colonies, have become impatient of colour, and it behoves every right-minded man and woman to think twice before he or she jumps to the conclusion that the Coloured people are a menace and that, therefore, they ought to be got rid of with the greatest possible despatch." (*Ibid.*, pp 242-243).

And further: **"We hear nowadays a great deal of the segregation policy, as if it were possible to put people in water-tight compartments." (*Ibid.* p. 243).**

It is in this memorable speech that Gandhi puts forth his vision for the future South Africa: **"If we look into the future, is it not a heritage we have to leave to posterity, that all the different races commingle and produce a civilisation that perhaps the world has not yet seen?" (*CW*, Vol 8, p. 246).**

**By August 1908 the question of "Closer Union" of the South African colonies had begun to present itself. *The Transvaal Leader* reported that Gandhi, addressed the "Transvaal Closer Union Society" in Johannesburg on August 20, 1908. This was in the course of a discussion of a study by Mr Alfred Barker on "The Asiatic Question In Relation to Closer Union". Gandhi made a significant speech presaging a vision for the emerging South African nation. He said: "The people who had settled in South Africa had laid down certain conditions under which the nation that was now forming had to live. Was it possible then to eradicate from one's mind the problem of Asiatic residence? It was a very interesting and instructive study; but it passed his comprehension that in all the papers he had read from the pens of those who had made South Africa their home they had never taken into consideration what the feelings of the Asiatics or of the Natives themselves might be. What would they have to say to any solution that was suggested for their acceptance? Was it suggested that the Asiatics or the Coloured races must perforce accept any solution which was found for their treatment by the predominant race – the European race? He ventured to suggest that if they ever adopted that policy it was doomed to failure. It was possible, perhaps, for one, two, or three years to follow a policy of that nature; but he was certain they would find that**

**both the Asiatics and the Natives would demand to be consulted with reference to their disposition. It was impossible to conceive that those races would ever allow the predominant race to dispose of them just as they chose." (*The Transvaal Leader*, August 21, 1908, *CW*, Vol 8, p. 466).**

**In a sense Gandhi may be said to have noticed both the emerging scaffolding of the apartheid regime and foretold its unworkability, if not collapse.**

Speaking in Durban on September 30, 1908, Gandhi made some perceptive and prescient remarks on the unification of South Africa. *The Natal Mercury* of October 1, 1908 reported his statement: "This was a question he had answered before a meeting of the Closer Union Society that had been formed in Johannesburg. He there stated that a United South Africa meant for British Indians greater restriction of their liberty, unless a unified South Africa meant unification not only of the white races, but of all British subjects, whether Coloured or white, who had chosen South Africa as their permanent home." (*CW*, Vol 9, p. 78). Incidentally, this seems almost to anticipate the famous words of the Freedom Charter adopted nearly half a century later by the Congress of the People, Kliptown, Johannesburg, June 25-26, 1955: "That South Africa belongs to all who live in it..."

According to *The Natal Mercury*'s report, Gandhi added in his Durban speech on September 30, 1908: " He could not conceive how the Imperial Government could possibly look with approval upon a scheme of unification which would mean the reduction of Asiatics and Natives to a state practically of slavery." (*CW*, Vol 9, p. 78). This apprehension was also, unfortunately, to be borne out by history.

An article by the writer Olive Schreiner in 1908 in *The Transvaal Leader* arguing against racial prejudice and envisaging a non-racist South Africa, was reprinted with some editorial appreciation in

Gandhi's journal. Schreiner wrote: "We cannot hope ultimately to equal the men of our own race living in more wholly enlightened and humanised communities, if our existence is passed among millions of non-free subjected peoples." ('Olive Schreiner' on Colour, *Indian Opinion*, January 2, 1909).

Gandhi's tendency to integrate observation and opinion with personal conduct meant that the one marched in step with the other. Early in the year 1909, Gandhi referred to the need for avoidance as far as possible of tea, coffee and cocoa, which "are produced through the labour of men who work more or less in conditions of slavery". Cocoa, he observed, was produced in the Congo where indentured Africans were "made to work beyond all limits of endurance". (From Gujarati *Indian Opinion*, January 9, 1909, *CW*, Vol 9, p. 136). This was a theme to which he was to return.

In the midst of the passive resistance campaign, the *Rand Daily Mail* voiced the fear: "Let it be seen that passive resistance can carry the day, and there will spring up men among the coloured people and the natives eager to achieve the success of Mr Gandhi." (Reproduced in *Indian Opinion*, January 30, 1909). In its next issue Gandhi's journal reported on the formation of the Transvaal Native Union in 1909. (*Indian Opinion*, February 6, 1909). A few months later the appearance of a "new journalistic compeer", A.P.O, the organ of the African Political Organisation, established to voice the concerns of the Coloured people, was welcomed by *Indian Opinion*. (*Indian Opinion*, May 29, 1909). The African Political Organisation later came to be known as the African People's Organisation.

The question of the Passive Resistance campaigns affecting the Africans evidently arose repeatedly and Gandhi dealt with it again in a speech at Germiston on June 7, 1909: "The Colonists would, therefore, see that no exception could be taken to Indians making use of this force in order to obtain a redress of their grievances.

Nor could such a weapon, if used by the Natives, do the slightest harm. On the contrary, if the Natives could rise so high as to understand and utilize this force, there would probably be no native question left to be solved." (*Indian Opinion*, June 12, 1909, *CW*, Vol 9, p. 244). Four years after this, African women in the Orange Free State did in fact take to passive resistance.

By 1909, the Indian interaction with the Africans was open and for all to see, though usually not overtly political. *Indian Opinion* reported of John Dube's institution in June 1909: "The Ohlange Industrial School, Phoenix, provided on Saturday last a musical treat of no mean order. Boys hailing from the coastal districts were competing for musical honours contested by those coming from the up-country districts, including Basutoland, and far away Matabeleland. The initiative displayed by the scholars was remarkable" (Native Scholars' Initiative, *Indian Opinion*, June 19, 1909). A second section of the same report was about another African institution in the neighbourhood of Phoenix: "On Thursday last the Inanda Mission for native girls provided an instance of perfect training in vocal music. This is a very old institution, the Principal, Mrs Edwards, having been connected with the Mission for over forty years. Mrs Hitchcock, one of the teaching staff, had trained a hundred girls to a high state of efficiency…".* (*Idem*)

A couple of months after the Germiston speech, Gandhi pursued the passive resistance theme with Dr Abdurrahman, the leader of the Coloured people, when the two were together lobbying support in Britain. He wrote to Dr Abdurrahman, who had in South Africa formed the African People's Organisation (APO), of the "inherent justice" of Dr Abdurrahman's cause. Gandhi's letter to Dr Abdurrahman, a grandson of a freed slave, was a call to passive resistance:

---

*Social contacts between the Phoenix Settlement and Africans in Inanda are referred to by C. F. Andrews in "Mr. Gandhi at Phoenix" in *The Modern Review*, Calcutta, May 1914 and in his other writings.

**"...you expected something from the Parliament or the British public, but why should you expect anything from them, if you expect nothing from yourself.**

**I promised to send you Thoreau's *Duty of Civil Disobedience.* I have not been able to procure it; I am writing for it today and hope to send it before you are off.**

**All I can add is a prayer that you may have the strength for it and ability to continue the work in South Africa along internal reform, and, therefore, passive resistance, even though, in the beginning, you may be only a handful." (August 23, 1909, *CW*, Vol 9, pp. 365-6).**

## V

### Against Segregation: "If South Africans are to become a real nation...."

New Year's Day, 1910 dawned with Gandhi's denunciation of the treatment meted out to an African boy by the Pretoria Town Council. The boy was earlier seated with other boys in the Town Hall during their examination. The Council was enraged by the seating arrangement and told the examiners that the hall would not be provided to them in future. The examiners then sought a separate room for the African. The Council refused this as well. Gandhi records in *Indian Opinion* that a resolution was passed by the Council that no African "or any other Coloured person should ever be allowed to use the Town Hall or any of its rooms". The atmosphere of the time may be gauged from the fact that according to Gandhi: "The whites who passed this resolution are counted very respectable and well-educated men." (*Indian Opinion*, January 1, 1910, *CW*, Vol 10, p. 113). "In a country like this", he continued, "the Coloured people are placed in an extremely difficult position. We think there is no way out of this except satyagraha. Such instances of injustice are a natural consequence of the whites' refusal to treat the Coloured people as their equals. It is in order to put an end to this state of affairs that we have been fighting in the Transvaal, and it is not surprising that the fight against a people with such deep prejudice should take a long time [to bear fruit]." (*Idem*).

Later the same month Gandhi quoted appreciatively G.K Chesterton's protest against an incident in Egypt where, in Chesterton's words, a "few harmless peasants at Denshawai* objected to the looting of their property; they were tortured and hanged." (*Indian Opinion*, January 22, 1910, *CW*, Vol 10, p.134). **In this article, Gandhi criticised the system "in which a few men capture power in the name of the people and abuse it. The people are deceived because it is under cover of their name that these men act."** (*Ibid*, p.135).

In the same year the Coloured people in the Cape, who had earlier had the franchise, faced effective disfranchisement by the South Africa Act. (*Indian Opinion*, February 26, 1910, *CW*, Vol 10, p. 165) Coloured people were effectively excluded from the Parliament of the Union and could only elect whites to represent them. When the leader of the Coloured people, Dr Abdurrahman, therefore made a protest on the occasion of the visit of the Prince of Wales to Cape Town in 1910, Gandhi fully supported the protest. Dr Abdurrahman said: "No Coloured man, I hope, will sing 'God Save the King' on that day. I know I won't. No Coloured man will see the Prince of Wales coming through the streets on that day and feel happy; for he will know it is the consummation of the robbing him of something he has had for 50 years." (Quoted in *Indian Opinion*, February 26, 1910, *CW*, Vol 10, p. 167). Complimenting Dr Abdurrahman, Gandhi wrote:

---

* Danishwai

"These words of Dr Abdurrahman, though bitter, are justified. The proposal was, of course, passed, but his words will be remembered for ever. If the other Coloured people were to follow in his footsteps, they would win redress of their grievances soon enough. We see no disloyalty in the Doctor's remarks. True loyalty may be bitter sometimes. It is not loyalty to say 'yes' to everything. True loyalty consists in expressing only what is in one's mind and acting accordingly." (*Indian Opinion*, February 26, 1910, *CW*, Vol 10, p. 167).

"Our struggle", wrote Gandhi a few days later, "is producing a profound effect on the Coloured people. Dr Abdurrahman has commented on it in his journal at great length and has held up the example of the Indian community to every Coloured person. Some of them have also passed a resolution in Johannesburg to defy the laws of the Government and take to satyagraha." (*Indian Opinion*, March 5, 1910, *CW*, Vol 10, p. 173)

In April 1910 Gandhi protested against the removal of Indian and African employees from the Johannesburg municipality. Calling it a "War Against Colour", Gandhi wrote: "The Johannesburg Municipality is being goaded into removing every Indian and Native employee, no matter how faithful his services may be and no matter what their length. That the Municipality or any other Department may not take a fresh supply of Coloured or Asiatic servants is a position against which not much can be said, but a summary dismissal of those who are already in its employ can do credit neither to the Municipality nor to those who force its hands." (*Indian Opinion*, April 2, 1910, *CW*, Vol 10, p. 200). He continued: "There can be no doubt that a ruthless removal of Asiatic and more especially Native servants will only end in disaster, but it behoves British Indians and other Asiatics, as also the Natives, to learn the needful lesson from the present activity against Asiatic and Coloured races. The latter must not rely upon the white Colonists finding work for them or giving it to them. **They will have to find independent means of earning a livelihood, and once a few**

**leaders set themselves towards solving the problem, it will be found exceedingly easy." (*Idem*).**

This presaged the emphasis on economic self-reliance and non-dependence that he was to place in the course of the freedom struggle in India.

Colour prejudice manifested itself again later the same month in Pretoria, inducing Gandhi's reproach: "This notorious municipality keeps up its reputation for waging war against Colour. A private Bill introduced during the last session of the Transvaal Parliament seeks to perpetuate the Town Regulations of the Boer regime which prevent the use of footpaths by Natives, Coloured people and Asiatics. The British Indian Association of the Transvaal has done well in formally protesting against the Bill. It contains, as it ought to, a clause to the effect that it will not come into force unless and until His Majesty* has expressed his pleasure not to disallow it. Lord Crewe** has now an opportunity of showing that he is ready to protect the unrepresented classes in South Africa from insult and molestation. But the ultimate court of appeal is and must be the people themselves who are affected by hostile legislation." (*Indian Opinion*, April 30, 1910, *CW*, Vol 10, p. 237).

In the midst of all this the Union of South Africa came into being on June 1, 1910.

As Gandhi pondered this development, he aired his concerns: "What is this Union? Whom does it unite? What does it unite? Or is it a Union against the Indian and other Coloured races inhabiting South Africa? (*Indian Opinion*, June 4, 1910, *CW*, Vol 10, p. 265).

Earlier, the Zulu chief Dinuzulu had been tried and convicted on various counts of high treason. He was defended by W P Schreiner,

---

* i.e., the King of England.

** The then Secretary of State for the Colonies.

a famous lawyer based in the Cape whose sister, the writer Olive Schreiner, became a deeply valued friend of Gandhi. In 1909 Gandhi had complimented W. P. Schreiner, when both were on a visit to London, for his "noble and self-sacrificing work in connection with the welfare of the coloured races of South Africa under the Draft South Africa Act" [Letter to W P Schreiner, July 24,1909, *CW*, Vol 95, (Supplementary Volume V), p. 5]. Dinuzulu, who was serving a term in prison was discharged soon after the formation of the Union of South Africa.

John Dube and Martin Luthuli, both to be among the founders of the South African Native National Congress (later African National Congress) , had close links with Dinuzulu. Martin Luthuli had been Dinuzulu's secretary. (See Freda Troup, *South Africa: An Historical Introduction*, Penguin Books, Harmondsworth, 1975, p. 208). And Dube had been, as recorded in the John Dube Museum at Ohlange in Inanda, an adviser to Dinuzulu.

Welcoming the discharge of Dinuzulu, Gandhi wrote: " It was no doubt right and proper that the birth of the Union should have been signalised for the Natives of South Africa by the clemency of the Crown towards Dinuzulu. Dinuzulu's discharge will naturally fire the imagination of the South African Natives. Will it not be equally proper to enable the Asiatics in South Africa to feel that there is a new and benignant spirit abroad in South Africa by conceding their demands, which are held, I make bold to say, to be intrinsically just by nine out of every ten intelligent Europeans in this Continent?" (*Indian Opinion*, June 11, 1910, *CW*, Vol 10, p. 263).

A little later the African leader, Rev. Dr Walter Rubusana, (who was later to be a Vice President of the ANC or the South African Native National Congress, as it was initially known, in January 1912) was elected to the Cape Provincial Council. Gandhi warmly welcomed his election to the Provincial Council. Anomalously, however, the colour provisions of the latest Union legislation had made Dr Rubusana ineligible to sit in the Union Parliament.

Gandhi warned against such legislative anomalies on which the Colonialists were seeking to build the South African nation; he said such provisions would prevent South Africa from becoming a "real nation":

**"The election of the Rev. Dr Rubusana as a member of the Cape Provincial Council for Tembuland by a majority of 25 over his two opponents is an event of great importance. The election is really a challenge to the Union Parliament with reference to the colour clause. That Dr Rubusana can sit in the Provincial Council but not in the Union Parliament is a glaring anomaly which must disappear if South Africans are to become a real nation in the near future. We congratulate Dr Rubusana and the Coloured races on his victory and trust that his career in the Council will do credit to him and those he represents." (*Indian Opinion*, September 24, 1910, *CW*, Vol 10, p. 325).**

Dr Rubusana, eleven years Gandhi's senior, had been educated at Lovedale to which reference was made above. Earlier, in 1909, Dr Rubusana, Dr Abdurrahman , Tengo Jabavu, Gandhi and others had been together in the gallery of the House of Lords in London on July 27, 1909 when the draft South Africa Act was debated. (See ES Reddy, *Gandhiji's Vision of a Free South Africa*, Sanchar Publishing House, New Delhi, 1995, p. 74, note 71).

Sometime later yet another form of discrimination attracted Gandhi's notice. Indian traders were forbidden by the Government in the Cape from entering the African areas. A report from Karreedouw indicated that only white traders are allowed to enter African districts like Transkei, "which are under the jurisdiction of the Cape" and that these traders "rob the Kaffirs". Gandhi advised the Cape Indians to inquire into the matter, write to the Government about it, ask for the ground on which entry is prohibited and that the "matter should not be left there". (*Indian Opinion*, November 5, 1910, *CW*, Vol 10, p. 345).

By March 1911 a new Immigration Bill was before Parliament. The campaigns had, it seemed, made some dent and the fear of the passive resistance idea spreading was ever present. Gandhi was able to record that a legislator "who at one time used to hold out threats against us, now says that General Smuts would do well to satisfy the Asiatics. The gentleman is afraid lest satyagraha spread to the whole of South Africa". (*Indian Opinion*, March 18, 1911, *CW*, Vol 10, p. 472).

The Gandhi-inspired British Indian Association in the Transvaal protested on May 1, 1911 against laws which would have the effect of bringing about what they described as "effectual compulsory segregation". (*CW*, Vol 11. p. 53). Legislation enacted in 1908 in the Transvaal had prohibited Europeans in what were described as "proclaimed areas" from " subletting any rights to Coloured persons and the acquisition of any rights whatsoever by the latter in such areas" (See *CW*, Vol 11, p. 54n). The effect of this legislation came to be manifested in 1911 when certain notices began to be issued to European owners who had sublet their property in Klerksdorp.

Among the various achievements of Satyagraha Gandhi noted in the *Indian Opinion* of June 3, 1911, was that: "The Railway regulations which were promulgated in the Transvaal, making distinctions between whites and Coloureds, were repealed and substituted by regulations of general application." (*CW*, Vol 11, p. 101).

Gandhi underlined a plain fact of production relations in South Africa:

"We all live upon the great industry of the Natives and Indians engaged in useful occupations in this country. In this sense they are more civilised than any of us, not excluding European non-producers, inhabiting this continent. Every speculator may leave the country; every lawyer may shut down his office, every merchant may wind up his business; and yet we should live comfortably on this land endowed by nature with a beneficent climate. **But if the great Native races were to stop work for a week, we should probably be starving. It must, then, be a privilege for us to be able to copy their productive industry and their ability as masters of useful handicraft."** (*Indian Opinion,* July 15, 1911, *CW,* Vol 11, pp. 124-125)

The same issue of *Indian Opinion,* referred also to the situation in Latin America where "it is more than probable that at least one-third of the Brazilian whites have negro blood in their veins." Nilo Pecanha who had attained the office of President in Brazil, was described as "a very swarthy man with curly hair... believed to be a coloured man". It was noted that "the coloured element" in Brazil, according to Harry Johnston, "enters all careers, serves in all trades, professions and employments in Brazil, from the humblest to nearly the highest....At least, it is said, that more than one of the chief magistrates of the 'United States of Brazil' has had a drop of Ethiopia in his veins". (*Indian Opinion,* July 15, 1911).

Meanwhile, preparations leading up to the birth of the African National Congress had begun. Pixley Seme, who had returned from his studies abroad to start law practice in Johannesburg, supplied the new energy that was needed.

Later that month, Gandhi's *Indian Opinion* informed its readers, relying on a *Mercury* telegram: "Preliminary arrangements have been completed...for the union of the various native associations throughout South Africa and a congress of the new organisation will be held next month." (A Native Union: The Lessons of the Passive Resistance Movement, *Indian Opinion,* July 29, 1911) It was expected at this stage that Dr Rubusana was to be the President of the new organisation.

*Indian Opinion* referred to "Seme, a young Zulu attorney practising at Johannesburg", as the "hon. Treasurer of the new society." (*Idem*)

Seme was quoted as saying: "We will discuss questions affecting the status of natives as a whole, such as the Pass Law." (*Idem*).

July 1911 was also significant for the First Universal Races Congress held in London. *Indian Opinion* had in its columns been mentioning plans for such a conference since as early as 1909 (as, for example in *Indian Opinion*, June 12, 1909 and April 16, 1910). Dr W E B DuBois, who was later known as the pioneering force behind the Pan-African movement, was among the participants as were Dr Rubusana, John Tengo Jabavu and Gandhi's mentor in India, the statesman Gopal Krishna Gokhale and Gandhi's associate, Henry Polak. One contribution to the deliberations was from M. Jean Finot of France whose work, "*Race Prejudice*", Gandhi apparently recommended to another earlier in the year, in April, and would refer to again in India.

In the following month, *Indian Opinion* published a note signed "Observer", perhaps from Polak or from Ms A A Smith who wrote with that pseudonym: "I had the pleasure of hearing Dr Du Bois.... He is the gifted author of the *Souls of Black Folk* .... and everyone will rejoice that the negroes have so able and far-seeing a representative; his spirit is co-operation and conciliation" (*Indian Opinion*, August 5, 1911).

Elsewhere, Dr DuBois wrote in an article published on August 24, 1911 that "there is good reason to affirm with Finot in the brochure which he gave to the congress: 'The conception of races as of so many watertight compartments into which human beings can be crammed as if they were so many breeds of horses or cattle, has had its day.' " [W E B DuBois, The First Universal Races Congress, in Eric J. Sundquist (ed.), *The Oxford W E B DuBois Reader* Oxford University Press, New York, 1996, p. 59]. Gandhi expected only indirect benefit for India from the conference. (Letter dated August 25, 1911, *CW*, Vol 11, p. 152). Even so, Gandhi's *Indian Opinion* on its front page hailed the "Great Universal Races Congress held in London", referring to it as "A Parliament of Man". (*Indian*

*Opinion*, August 26, 1911). It referred again to DuBois as "one of the best known authorities on the negro problem". Dr DuBois's interview to the *Manchester Guardian* was quoted at great length. He had said, *inter alia*: "Further the American people find a justification for their treatment of the Negro in the attitude of England and Germany to the dark races in their colonies. They quote England as holding the opinion that the dark races must be kept in a condition of eternal tutelage, and they point to the political subservience of the Indian races under your government " (*Idem*).

A full page report of Polak's speech at the Universal Races Congress, in which he referred also to the passive resistance struggle of "the Transvaal Asiatics", was published on the front page of *Indian Opinion*, September 9, 1911. The *Indian Opinion* issues of September 2, and September 9, 1911 also carried long reports of the proceedings by A Chessel Piquet. And in the September 9, 1911 report the contributions of Tengo Jabavu and Dr Rubusana and of Dr DuBois were highly praised. The latter report noted: "Dr Du Bois is not only a great man amongst negroes, but also a great man amongst the world's great men".

Chessel Piquet's report in *Indian Opinion* stressed the larger long-term implications of the Congress as the reason for the discouragement it received from British officialdom: "Indians were compelled to realise that the British Government — a 'Liberal' government — did not officially recognise the Congress (though its Vice Presidents included both the Prime Minister and the Leader of the Opposition) almost entirely because of the objections raised by the reactionary elements of the India Office, who, not unnaturally, felt that, if the British Government formally accepted the conclusions which it was known the Congress would be called upon to formulate, the whole fabric of modern Imperialism and all that it connotes would be rent asunder". (A Chessel Piquet, The First Universal Races Congress, *Indian Opinion*, September 2, 1911)

The *Indian Opinion* issue of October 21, 1911 carried extracts from an article, "*The Coloured Man in Art and Letters*", by Duse Mahomed, the famous author of "*In the Land of the Pharoahs*". Duse Mahomed had referred to many authors of mixed blood, saying that "a race capable of producing a Poushkin, a Dumas, and a Dunbar in letters, and a Coleridge Taylor and a Marion Cook in music, can neither be lacking in high intellect and artistic temperament nor devoid of that dash of creative genius without which literature is debased to the level of nonsensical drivel and music degraded to a flaccid medley of conventional sounds." Duse Mahomed was an Egyptian of Sudanese origin.

As *Indian Opinion* noted of the personalities mentioned, all had African blood in them. Paul Dunbar, the famous African-American author, "was of pure African lineage" while the others were of mixed blood. According to information culled from Duse Mahomed, Alexander Dumas was said to have "descended from an African grandmother in Haiti", Alexander Pushkin "had an Ethiopian grandmother", Samuel Coleridge Taylor was "the son of a West African doctor", and Will Marion Cook had "both maternal and paternal African forbears".

A headline in the same issue of *Indian Opinion* described as "A Notable Conference" a meeting of African women that had taken place in Potchefstroom. The week-long conference, which had been attended by at least 150 women from various parts of South Africa, had been "assembled under the auspices of the Native Women's Christian Union (of which Mrs Amos Burnet is president)". The object was "to consult over matters affecting the future well-being of their class."

There were some African workers on the Tolstoy Farm settlement for the passive resisters, which Gandhi and Hermann Kallenbach had established not far from Lawley Station. Gandhi observed to Kallenbach that the Africans on the Farm should "feel that here they may depend upon the fairest treatment. And I have no doubt that if it proceeds from the heart and is uniform, continuous and not from affectation, it will bless both the parties." [Letter to Kallenbach, November 6, 1911, *CW*, Vol 96, (Supplementary Vol VI), p. 89]

**The South African Native National Congress (later renamed the African National Congress) was founded in January 1912.**

**Gandhi's *Indian Opinion* welcomed the event as "The Awakening of the Natives" and wrote: "Our friend and neighbour, the Rev. John L. Dube, Principal of the Ohlange Native Industrial School, has received the high honour of being elected the first President of the newly-inaugurated Inter-State Native Congress." (*Indian Opinion*, February 10, 1912). The journal expressed appreciation of the manifesto issued by John Dube "to his countrymen" and published extracts from it. The extracts from Dube's manifesto concluded: "We have been distinguished by the world as a race of born gentlemen – a truly glorious title, bestowed on few other peoples – and by the gentleness of our manners (poor though we may be, unlettered and ill-clad), and by the nobility of our character shall we break down the adamantine wall of colour prejudice and force even our enemies to be our admirers and our friend." (*Idem*).**

**The formation of such an organisation had already been presaged in the report, referred to above, that *Indian Opinion* had carried more than five months earlier (*Indian Opinion*, July 29, 1911).**

Gandhi criticised the racist policies bearing on public health which had "meant death and destruction to the Native people of this country." (*Indian Opinion*, April 6, 1912, *CW*, Vol 11, p. 254). He cited the evidence before the Tuberculosis Commission given by Dr Thornton, the Medical Officer of Health for the Cape Province. In this article Gandhi noted: "Anyone who has visited a Location, whether Native or Indian, must be impressed with the utter hopelessness of such places. The shameful neglect of the roadways, the utter absence of proper drainage, and the wretched condition of the buildings, all show at once that this is a Location – a place where Coloured people are condemned to spend their days as outcasts." (*Ibid.* p. 255). He opposed the Johannesburg Town Council's proposed policy under which Africans "who are at present living where they please are to be rounded up into a huge compound, where they will be compelled to live, whether they like it or not. A fence is to be erected around the Location, and the 'inmates' (suggestive term) are to enter through the gateway, which will be under police guard. At a certain hour the gates will be closed, and opened again in time to allow the Natives to get to work for their European masters". (*Idem*).

Gandhi continues his criticism of the proposed segregation with a sarcasm not often found in his writings: "A well-known Johannesburg citizen gave it as his opinion that the scheme would be a great success, not only from a public-health point of view, but also from a police point of view. Now, as for the public health point of view, we are quite certain that the public referred to is the white public and not the public which is to receive the special advantage of living in this municipal compound; and we think that Dr Thornton will agree with us. And what, pray, is the 'police point of view'? We think we can guess, but, as there can be no certainty about it, we will content ourselves by merely suggesting that, by segregating all the blacks, it will then be an easy matter to keep a watchful eye upon the white criminal class which is known to congregate in the cities." (*Indian Opinion*, April 6, 1912, *CW*, Vol 11, pp. 236).

In August 1912 there was a smallpox epidemic in Johannesburg. Gandhi's first reaction was to warn the Indian community that "even if the epidemic did not originate this time with the Indians and though only a few cases appear to have occurred among them, they should not be any the less careful in the matter." (*Indian Opinion*, August 17, 1912, *CW*, Vol 11, p. 305). He warned that there would, in this context, be demands for segregation of the various communities, which would be difficult to resist and asked Indians to cooperate fully with the medical authorities. (*Idem*).

But a week later Gandhi spoke out against segregation even in the context of the small pox outbreak. He told *The Transvaal Leader*: "Segregation would in any case be totally ineffective. Even if you kept the Indians in one district, the Eurafricans in another, you could not prevent them intermixing outside in the ordinary course of their business. Segregation would not remove the danger of infection." (*The Transvaal Leader*, August 23, 1912, *CW*, Vol 11, p. 306). "The proper way", he continued, " of dealing with all classes of the community, European, Asiatic, Eurafrican and Native, is to allow them freedom of movement, subject to a strict supervision as regards health conditions." (*Ibid.*, pp 306-7). He reiterated his repeated opposition to class legislation: "In any case, I am convinced that the Imperial Government would not sanction any class legislation such as a policy of segregation would entail." (*Ibid.*, p. 307; see also *Ibid.*, p. 290n).

**The eminent Indian leader, Gopal Krishna Gokhale visited South Africa in October- November 1912. Gandhi acted as the main organiser of the tour and Gokhale's escort in the course of it. The historic confluence between John Dube, Gopal Krishna Gokhale and Gandhi, to which reference has already been made, took place in November 1912. Gandhi had praised Dube in print in 1905 and his journal had welcomed the choice of Dube as the President-General of the South African Native National Congress (later renamed African National Congress) established in January 1912. On November 11, 1912, Gokhale was taken by Gandhi to meet John Dube at the Ohlange Institute near Phoenix and discuss the "Native question". (See E S Reddy, *Gandhiji's Vision of a Free South Africa*, op. cit., p. 22). Gokhale received a warm welcome from the staff and students of Dube's school. The occasion is surcharged with historical significance. Eight decades before the complete**

**liberation of South Africa, a past and a future President of the Indian National Congress, (Gokhale had been President of the Congress in 1905; Gandhi became President in 1924), were calling on the leader of the African National Congress.**

***Indian Opinion*** **reported: "Mr Gokhale then paid a visit to the Natal Industrial School at Ohlange and spent some time discussing the Native question with the Rev. John Dube, Principal of the School, and President of the Native Congress. The students sang a couple of Zulu songs and the band played popular music". (*****Indian Opinion*****, November 23, 1912).**

**Earlier, W P Schreiner and Dr Abdurrahman, among others, welcomed Gokhale in Cape Town. A meeting with Olive Schreiner took place en route to Kimberley (*****CW*****, Vol 11, p. 612). Her novel, "*****The Story of an African Farm*****", was among the books sold at Phoenix (See, for example, *****Indian Opinion*****, June 17, 1914).**

**Among those who welcomed Gokhale in Kimberley was Isaac Joshua, Chairman of the local branch of the African Political Association*. Joshua said that "the coloured people of South Africa laboured under great disabilities, and they sympathised with the Indians. Their fight was our fight, because they laboured under the same obnoxious laws as they (the coloureds) laboured under, and he only trusted that the Indians might receive better treatment in future through the visit of Mr Gokhale, and that following that, the coloured people in South Africa would also receive fair and just treatment, as they should under British rule." [*****Indian Opinion, Souvenir of the Hon. Gopal Krishna Gokhale's Tour in South Africa, October 22nd – November 18, (1912)*** **pp. 8-9].**

---

*The word used in the news reports is "Association" rather than "Organisation".

The condition of plantation workers in Africa continued to receive Gandhi's attention. He wrote: "In cocoa plantations, Negro workers are subjected to such inhuman treatment that if we witnessed it with our own eyes we would have no desire to drink cocoa. Volumes have been written on the tortures inflicted in these plantations." (*Indian Opinion*, March 8, 1913, *CW*, Vol 11, p. 483). A couple of years earlier he had complained to his associate, H S L Polak, about "the abominable chocolate", calling it "that cursed product of devilish slave labour." [August 26, 1911, *CW*, Vol 96 (Supplementary Vol VI), p. 71].

At another place he had written during a voyage to England: " I also avoid tea and coffee as far as possible, since they are the produce of slave labour." (*Indian Opinion*, August 7, 1909, *CW*, Vol 9, pp. 277-8)

*Indian Opinion* gave prominence to a strong critique made by Senhore de Carvalho, a former Curator (official Protector of Africans) in Principe, Portuguese Africa, of Portugal's conduct and attitude towards the African population. In a leaflet issued by the Anti-Slavery Society, Senhore de Carvalho, who had resigned his position after investigating the facts, wrote alleging the existence of slavery in the colony: "....I speak of the labourers born in Angola. They are actual slaves. Caught in the interior, or sold to Europeans by their chiefs, they come down to the coast like any other sort of merchandise." ("Slavery in West Africa", *Indian Opinion*, April 26, 1913).

*Indian Opinion* noted that *The Spectator*, where the report was first published, had observed that de Carvalho's work appeared to "bear the stamp of genuineness" and also that it was "as regards the main fact of slavery, fully borne out by the first-hand evidence of Mr Nevinson, Mr Burtt, and Mr Harris."(*Idem*).

The African women's Anti-Pass struggles in the Orange Free State and the events leading to Indian women going to jail as part of

Indian passive resistance both had their origin in the first and second quarters of 1913 and the cross-fertilisation of ideas they represent are dealt with in the next section.

In the midst of these events, Gandhi's friend, associate and first biographer, Joseph J. Doke passed away in August 1913. Writing about him, Gandhi made a piercing social comment: "He died whilst finding further fields for his loving activity. And as he loved, so is his death today mourned by not only his European congregation, not only by Englishmen, but also by many of his Native, Chinese and Indian friends. In a place where even men of religion are not free from the local prejudice against colour, Mr Doke was among the few who know no distinction of race, colour or creed." (*Indian Opinion,* August 23, 1913), *CW*, Vol 12, p. 168).

**In the week following, *Indian Opinion* supported John Dube's criticism of the Natives Land Act passed by the Union Parliament. The Act sought to fortify White property rights. *Indian Opinion* commented: "The Natives Land Act of the Union Parliament has created consternation among the Natives. Indeed, every other question, not excluding the Indian question, pales into insignificance before the great Native question. This land is theirs by birth and this Act of confiscation – for such it is – is likely to give rise to serious consequences unless the Government take care." (*Indian Opinion*, August 30, 1913). The Act provided the basis for evictions and other hardships faced by the African population and set the tone for much of what followed in South Africa by defining "African reserves" and making precarious the rights of Africans on other lands in the country.**

**John Dube's appeal to the British public against the Act was carried also by *Indian Opinion*. Dube had said "We ask for freedom to purchase land wherever opportunities occur and our sparse means permit. We ask that we may be permitted to build for ourselves a home wheresoever a landlord is agreeable.**

**Who can affirm that our requests are unreasonable or impossible? .... You must know that every one of us has been born in this land, and we have no other. You must know that for untold generations this land was solely ours — long before your fathers had put a foot on our shores." (*Idem*)**

**Later in the year Solomon T Plaatje, who was General Secretary of the SANNC (later renamed ANC), wrote in the Lovedale journal, Christian Express, describing the Act as "a carefully prepared, deliberate and premeditated scheme to compass the partial enslavement of the Natives." (quoted in Maureen Rall, *Peaceable Warrior : The Life and Times of Sol T. Plaatje*, Sol Plaatje Educational Trust, Kimberley, 2003, p. 125).**

## VI

### Cross-Fertilisation of Ideas in South Africa: "womenfolk will join the struggle"

Gandhi's activities influenced and were in turn influenced by African opinion and politics. His own ideas on Africa and Africans evolved and expanded with extended experience in Africa.

The South African Native National Congress (later ANC) was, as noted above, founded in January 1912, an impetus having been provided also by the creation of the Union. As Albert Luthuli was to put it half a century later, the setting up of the Union meant that by "ganging up together, Boer and Briton had achieved their coup. It took us very little time to recognise that only by working for our own unity could we hope to withstand the effects, upon us and within us, of being treated like cattle..." (Albert Luthuli, *Let My People Go: An Autobiography*, Collins, London, 1962, p. 89).

Incidentally, the SANNC Constitution drawn up later, in 1919, had a clause (Clause 13 in Chapter IV) which emphasised "passive action" (Referred to by E S Reddy in *Gandhiji's Vision of A Free South Africa*, p. 75, note 85). It is of some interest to note that Richard W. Msimang (1884-1933), who "often served as the legal adviser" of the South African Native National Congress, is reputed to have been "primarily responsible" for drafting the Constitution of the SANNC in 1919 ( vide Timothy Keegan's introduction to a re-publication, circa 1996, of R. W. Msimang's rare booklet on the *Natives Land Act 1913: Specific Cases of Evictions and Hardships, etc*, first published soon after the enactment). Msimang was among the first students at John Dube's Ohlange Institute and was perhaps there when Gandhi set up camp right across at Phoenix. From 1910 Msimang, having meanwhile qualified as a lawyer in England, set up a legal practice in Johannesburg, where incidentally Gandhi had meanwhile moved.

While individual factors and threads may be points for further research, there appears to have been a general consensus within the organised African leadership in South Africa by this time that unity and peaceful action was the way to go forward.

The African Womens' Passive Resistance in the Orange Free State from June 1913 onwards is an example of an early cross-fertilisation of ideas between Gandhi and Africa.

**Gandhi's journal foregrounded its support for the African women's struggle in the Orange Free State with a full page article on the front page emblazoned with the banner heading "Native Women's Brave Stand" in capital letters (*Indian Opinion*, August 2, 1913), relying for its facts on the African newspaper *Abantu*. *Indian Opinion* had referred earlier to "Native Women Passive Resisters" noting, with the African Political Organisation, that one of the "most iniquitous" laws "is that of the Orange Free State which compels coloured and**

**Native females over the age of sixteen to carry passes. It has led to respectable Coloured women being locked up, and young native girls being dragged from their homes and cruelly outraged by policemen. It is not surprising therefore, to learn that the women of those municipalities where the Pass laws are enforced against them have decided to resist the law, and refuse to carry passes." (Native Women Passive Resisters, *Indian Opinion*, July 5, 1913).**

The question of passes required for African and Coloured women in the Orange Free State had come to a boil after the formation of the Union. Representations were of no avail. Julia Wells writes: "When these efforts brought no satisfactory result, the topic of passes for women quickly became a rallying point for the newly formed South African Natives National Congress (SANNC). Meeting in Bloemfontein in February 1912, the SANNC called on the Union Government to withdraw all provisions for passes for women. As if foreshadowing events to come, it also stressed the significance of the passive resistance campaign being successfully carried on by Mahatma Gandhi in the nearby Transvaal province. The African Political Organisation, representing the local Coloured population, also took up the issue of passes for women". [Julia Wells, "Passes and Bypasses: Freedom of Movement for African Women under the Urban Areas Act of South Africa" in Margaret Hay and Marcia Wright (eds) *African Women and the Law: Historical Perspectives*, Boston University Papers on Africa – VII, 1982, p. 130]

In relation to the Anti-Pass Campaign in the Orange Free State, 1913-20, Cherryl Walker writes of the campaign by African women provoked by an incident on June 6, 1913 when some women in Bloemfontein were arrested for not having passes: " This incident was the beginning of a widespread campaign of passive resistance, which spread to all the major Free State towns and involved hundreds of women. There is no indication that the Bloemfontein protesters had worked out a careful campaign beforehand, but once the first arrests had been made, there were definite attempts to turn a spontaneous outburst of feeling into a more co-ordinated demonstration of popular opposition. The women turned to the tactics of passive resistance and civil disobedience which the South African Indian Congress [SAIC] leader, M K Gandhi, had already pioneered in South Africa." (Cherryl Walker, *Women and Resistance in South Africa*, Second Edition; David Philip: Cape Town & Johannesburg/ Monthly Review Press, New York, 1982, p. 27).

Gandhi himself is said to have in turn been influenced by this struggle in focussing still further on involvement of women in the next round of his movement in South Africa. The movement was resumed in 1913 as the authorities failed to honour their commitment to repeal the tax on members of former indentured Indians' families and failed also to resolve the fresh issues which had arisen about the validity and recognition of Indian marriages. This followed upon Justice Searle's judgement in the Cape Supreme Court on March 14, 1913 in Bai Miriam's case. The judgement directly concerned Indian women as the status of most Indian marriages became questionable under the immigration law. Sixty years later, the anti-apartheid activist lawyer Albie Sachs, a future judge of the Constitutional Court in free South Africa, summed up the effect of this judgement: "that customary Indian marriages were legally invalid because they were potentially if not actually polygamous". (Albie Sachs, *Justice In South Africa*, University of California Press, Berkeley, 1973, p. 207). On March 30, 1913, a few weeks after the judgement, a mass meeting was held in Johannesburg to consider the effect of the Bai Miriam case. As Gandhi's wife Kasturba and others saw it, the judgement meant that all the married couples coming within its sweep were living in sin and all their children suddenly became illegitimate. On April 15, 1913 Gandhi asked for an amendment to Union law to legalise non-Christian marriages.

Sometime before April 19, 1913 Kasturba Gandhi decided to join the struggle and court arrest (see the chronology in *CW*, Volume 12, 1966 edition, pp. 646-8). On April 19 Gandhi informed the Indian statesman Gokhale of the decision:
"Most of the settlers here including the womenfolk will join the struggle. The latter feel that they can no longer refrain from facing gaol no matter what it may mean in a place like this. Mrs Gandhi made the offer on her own initiative and I do not want to debar her." (*CW*, Vol 12, p. 41). Ultimately Kasturba Gandhi, Valiamma and other Indian women were imprisoned in this movement. Indian women courted arrest from September 1913, after the African women in Orange Free State. Interestingly, Gandhi himself ended up in Bloemfontein prison, Orange Free State at the end of 1913. (Gandhi, *Satyagraha in South Africa*, Chapters 45 and 46).

At the end of September 1913, Dr Abdurrahman, in his presidential address to the annual conference of the African Political Organisation held at Kimberley, drew attention to the Indian struggle. In remarks that bring to mind the pointed suggestion Gandhi had made to him in August 1909, Dr Abdurrahman remarked that the method of passive resistance might usefully be emulated by (other) "coloured races".

Extracts from Dr Abdurrahman's speech were published by *Indian Opinion* around the time Gandhi was in Bloemfontein prison. In his speech Dr Abdurrahman had said: "If a handful of Indians, in a matter of conscience, can so firmly resist what they consider injustice, what could the coloured races not do if they were to adopt this practice of passive resistance?" (*Indian Opinion*, December 3, 1913).

*Indian Opinion* published also Dr Abdurrahman's remarks applauding the African women's struggle in the Orange Free State. (*Idem*). Sol T. Plaatje, General Secretary of the African National Congress, was also to include Dr Abdurrahman's Kimberley speech in Chapter 10 of his well-known work *Native Life in South Africa*, which was published some months later.

Gandhi was released from prison on December 18, 1913 and spoke three days later at a Durban meeting dressed as an indentured labourer. The Indian women, including his wife Kasturba began to be released soon thereafter.

Passive resistance, as reflected in the struggles of the African women in the Orange Free State and in the Indian struggles, had emerged in South Africa. Sheridan Johns III writes of the struggle led by the African National Congress in 1919 in the Transvaal: "Following the example of the women (and perhaps also that of the Indians led by Gandhi) the Transvaal section of the Congress called its first passive resistance campaign in March-April 1919. Upon the Witwatersrand, several thousand Africans defied the pass laws by turning in their required documents." [Thomas Karis and Gwendolen M. Carter (eds.) *From Protest To Challenge: A Documentary History of African Politics in South Africa 1882- 1964*; Volume 1: *Protest And Hope* 1882-1934 by Sheridan Johns III, Hoover Institution Press, Stanford University, Stanford, 1972, p. 65].

Another scholar describes the African passive resistance in the Transvaal in 1919 thus:
"After the war, Witwatersrand branches of the Congress, taking a leaf out of Gandhi's book, organised the collection of passes in sacks and persuaded thousands, without the use of picketing or physical force, to hand themselves over to the police for disobeying the law." (T R H Davenport, *South Africa: A Modern History*, Macmillan Press, London, 1977, p. 179). The 1919 movement was to be suppressed rather brutally and it was some time before passive resistance re-emerged in South Africa.

**On July 18, 1914, in a "farewell letter" on his final departure from South Africa after a stay of more than two decades, Gandhi endorsed what he described as the "theory" of the British Constitution "that there should be no legal racial inequality**

**between different subjects of the Crown, no matter how much practice may vary according to local circumstance." (*Indian Opinion*, July 29, 1914, *CW*, Vol 12, p. 502).**

Having set sail for England before returning to India, Gandhi wrote from his ship on July 23, 1914 recalling the fond farewells he and his party had received at several places: "The white people, too, made an excellent demonstration of their affection. During the final days, we drank the cup of their love also full to the brim. Occasions such as these prove that there is no bar or permanent division as between the whites and Coloureds and that, if both the sides make the required effort, the evil in South Africa can be overcome." (*Indian Opinion*, August 26, 1914, *CW*, Vol 12, p. 508).

Gandhi's concerns against oppression were, of course, not limited to Indians and Africans. Even within South Africa, they extend to the rights of Chinese miners (*CW*, Volume 5, pp 60-61), seeking equal protection for Chinese passive resisters as for Indian passive resisters in 1911 (*CW*, Vol 11, p. 49) and speaking out against the invidious distinction made in Transvaal legislation between Turkish Muslims and Christians (*CW*, Vol 7, p. 104).

Gandhi left something permanent behind him in South Africa – and what he left behind was for all South Africans. A decade after Gandhi's return to India in 1915, Sarojini Naidu, the famous Indian freedom fighter who later headed the Indian National Congress, visited South Africa. On February 29, 1924 she wrote to Gandhi from Johannesburg: " I cannot sleep in South Africa and it is all your fault. You haunt the land and its soil is impregnated with the memory of your wonderful struggle, sacrifice and triumph. I am so deeply moved, so deeply aware all the time that here was the cradle of satyagraha -- do you wonder that I have been able to move thousands of men and women in the last two days to tears under the influence and stimulus of your inspiration? .... I have seen your legion of old friends and followers – white, brown and black – the whole gamut of the polychromatic scale of humanity in this land — all send you their love...." [See Mrinalini Sarabhai (Ed) *The Mahatma And The Poetess*, Bharatiya Vidya Bhavan, Mumbai and Sarvodaya International Trust, Bangalore, 1998, pp. 37-38]

## VII

### After Return from Africa: no justice for Indians "if none is rendered to natives of the soil"

After his return to India, Gandhi remained in touch with African struggles and the state of civil liberties in Africa. In October 1920 he was in the midst of a struggle in India. But we find him commenting in *Young India*: "Look at the trial of an English officer and the farcical punishment he received for having deliberately tortured inoffensive Negroes at Nairobi." (*CW*, Vol 18, p 321).

Gandhi drew inspiration not only from his experiences in South Africa but also from his reading of the history of Africa as a whole. On one occasion in 1920, when asked to explain his movement for non-cooperation with British rule, he cited the example of Somaliland (Somalia) from the interior areas of which the British had evacuated in 1909-10. In an interview to *The Times of India*, reproduced in the journal *Young India* under the title "*Swaraj in Nine Months*", Gandhi said: "This movement is an endeavour to purge the present Government of the selfishness and greed which determine almost everyone of their activities. Suppose that we have made it impossible by dissociation from them to feed their greed. They might not wish to remain in India, as happened in the case of Somaliland, where, the moment its administration ceased to be a paying proposition they evacuated it." (*Young India*, December 29, 1920, *CW*, Vol 19,169).

In 1921 Gandhi wrote feelingly against "insolence, pride of race, religion or colour." (*Young India*, June 1, 1921, *CW*, Vol 20, p.159).

African- American interest in Gandhi's movements had also been aroused. In March -April 1919 Gandhi had called for a protest in India against the Rowlatt legislation sought to be introduced by the colonial regime. The legislation which envisaged arbitrary detention, and trials without effective legal assistance, cutting off pleadings and appeals, was a serious assault on democratic rights. The protest was followed on April 13, 1919 by the infamous Jallianwala Bagh Massacre in which an unarmed crowd in Amritsar, in northern India, was fired upon by British-led troops. In September 1919, the African-American political activist Hubert Harrison, considered the Father of Harlem Radicalism, writing in the *New Negro* under a pseudonym, condemned the Rowlatt legislation and described it elsewhere as "the rottenest legal terrorism that the modern world has yet seen". [Jeffrey B. Perry, (ed.) *A Hubert Harrison Reader*, Wesleyan University Press, Middletown, CT, 2001, p. 213].

In October 1921, a few days after Gandhi issued a manifesto for his movement of non-cooperation with the British regime, Harrison wrote that Gandhi, "stands out among men of all colours today as the greatest, most unselfish and powerful leader of the modern world." [Jeffrey B. Perry, (ed.) *op. cit.* p. 314]

In the same year, in an address in South Africa, Rev Zaccheus R. Mahabane, President of the Cape Province National Congress, expressly contemplated the possibility of Gandhian resistance. Mahabane warned: "… let no race or class or creed be driven to such a condition of despair as it might be compelled to adopt the Gandhian policy of 'non-co-operation' – taxation without representation leads to this." [Thomas Karis and Gwendolen Carter (eds.) *op. cit.*; Volume 1, p.296]. Mahabane was later, in 1924 and again in 1937-40, to be President General of the African National Congress. He was also the president of the Non-European Unity movement activated in 1943.

The urge to explore the possibilities of Gandhi-type methods was expressed regionally as well. In 1924 the eclectic James Thaele, a Lovedale product, who had later graduated in the United States, became, shortly after returning to South Africa, the President of the Western Cape Congress. "Periodically he argued for non-co-operation with the authorities and also referred to the Gandhian example of passive resistance." (Peter Walshe, *The Rise of African Nationalism in South Africa: The African National Congress 1912-1952*, University of California Press, Berkeley, 1971, p. 166).

Gandhi was in personal contact with leading African-American personalities like Dr W E B DuBois, the pioneer of the Pan-African movement, who was to spend his last days in Ghana. Dr DuBois had been repeatedly referred to in Gandhi's *Indian Opinion* in South Africa. In 1911 *Indian Opinion* had carried laudatory references to Dr DuBois and his role. Gandhi, for his part, had been referred to in the pages of Dr DuBois' journal, *Crisis*, since at least the early nineteen twenties. *Crisis*, a monthly journal from New York, was the organ of the National Association for the Advancement of Colored People (NAACP). In March 1922, the month in which Gandhi was to be arrested, *Crisis* carried a five-page long appreciative article on Gandhi. The *Crisis* article referred to the massacre in Amritsar in 1919 and set out in detail the content of Gandhi's non-co-operation and boycott movement. *Crisis* went on to observe: "The second outstanding factor in Mr Gandhi's program is the idea and practice of non-violence or passive resistance. Like the principle of non-co-operation, it kills without striking its adversary." (Gandhi and India, *Crisis*, New York, March 1922). Years later, writing in 1957, Dr DuBois was to recall that "(w)ith the First World War came my first knowledge of Gandhi". (W E B DuBois, Gandhi and the American Negroes, *Gandhi Marg*, Bombay, July 1957, Vol 1, Number 3, p.175) Referring to the NAACP, Dr DuBois wrote: "I remember the discussion we had on inviting Gandhi to visit America and how we were forced to conclude that this land was not civilized enough to receive a coloured man as an honoured guest." (*Idem*).

Gandhi sent Dr DuBois a "love message" for *Crisis* on May 1, 1929.

Marcus Garvey too was in touch with Gandhi. Garvey, Chairman of the Fourth Annual International Convention of the Negro Peoples of the World, had on behalf of "the Negroes of the world" sent greetings to Gandhi for the "fight for the freedom of your people and country". Garvey added: "We are with you". Gandhi, who had been released in early 1924 after spending nearly two years in prison, said "I gladly publish and gratefully acknowledge" Garvey's message, which was carried by him in *Young India* on August 21, 1924 with the following comment:
"Theirs is perhaps a task more difficult than ours. But they have some very fine workers among them. They have fine physique. They have a glorious imagination. They are as simple as they are brave. M. Finot has shown by his scientific researches that there is in them no inherent inferiority as is commonly supposed to be the case. All they need is opportunity. I know that if they have caught the spirit of the Indian movement, their progress must be rapid." (*CW*, Vol 25, p. 26). Incidentally, M Finot's was a work to which Gandhi had referred even during his South Africa days. (See letters to L. W. Ritch, April 12 and 18, 1911 *CW*, Vol 11, p. 22 and p. 29).

Later in 1924 Gandhi commented on the case of Harry Thuku of Kenya who was described by C F Andrews as "one of the brightest lads I had seen" in East Africa. Thuku, who had protested against the flogging to death of some of his countrymen and against forced labour by African unmarried girls on plantations of white settlers, was detained without trial and deported to Kisumayu. Gandhi described Thuku as the victim of "lust for power" and wrote that if Thuku "ever saw these lines, he will perhaps find comfort in the thought that even in distant India many will read the story of his deportation and trials with sympathy." (*Young India*, December

18, 1924, *CW*, Vol 25, p. 398). Thuku, a telephone operator in Nairobi, had taken to the politics of protest by forming the "Young Kikuyu Association". (See Basil Davidson, *Africa In History: Themes And Outlines*, Paladin Books, Granada Publishing, St Albans, 1974, p. 298). This had soon become the East African Association, gaining wide membership and spearheading strikes by the growing working class in Kenya. Interestingly, Thuku had been arrested in March 1922, five days after Gandhi's own arrest in India. The colonialists had been evidently worried and a Church of Scotland missionary at Kikuyu "warned friends in London of the growing African unrest and wrote that Thuku was trying to become the Gandhi of Kenya." (Robert G. Gregory, *India and East Africa: A History of Race Relations within the British Empire 1890-1939*, Clarendon Press, Oxford, 1971, p. 216).

Gandhi, along with Andrews, had also repudiated the suggestion floated by Sir Theodore Morison of the India Office, among others, for reserving German East Africa for administration by the Government of India. (Gregory, *op. cit.* pp. 173-174, pp. 192-193, p. 217, pp 280-281, pp 503-504). Andrews arrived in Mombasa, Kenya on December 1, 1919. And by December 4, he was able to inform Gandhi that the local Indian Congress leaders were prepared to dissociate themselves from the idea. (Hugh Tinker, *The Ordeal of Love: C F Andrews and India*, Oxford University Press, Delhi, 1979, p. 162). The Imperial Indian Citizenship Association published a memorandum authored by C F Andrews on the subject. Andrews wrote of the suggestion made by Sir Theodore Morison that "Mahatma Gandhi himself was opposed to it." [*Indian Quarterly Register* (republished as *Indian Annual Register*), 1925, Vol 1, p. 371]

That was consistent with the attitude that Gandhi sought to inculcate. Earlier, in March 1924, Gandhi had been approached by Mahadeo Panday and Caramat Alli Macdoom who wrote to him about the prospect of an African influx in British Guiana (now Guyana) in

South America and that the Africans were seeking the same entitlements as were offered to Indians there. Gandhi, who was then convalescing in Bombay after a surgery, replied on March 28, 1924: "You state that the Negroes are clamouring for the conditions offered to our Indian colonists. Personally I do not mind it, nor need our countrymen in British Guiana fear the proposed influx of the Negroes. If the 1,30,000 Indians give a good account of themselves, they will bless themselves and bless the Negroes and everyone else who goes there." (*CW*, Vol 23, p.332).

A delegation from South Africa led by Gandhi's old friend Dr Abdurrahman visited India in 1925. It was present at the Kanpur session of the Indian National Congress, which was also addressed by Dr Abdurrahman. When Gandhi spoke at the session he criticised South African Europeans for their policies but also referred to his friendships with individuals among them. In this context he mentioned in particular "that great poetess and philanthropist and that most self-effacing woman – Olive Schreiner." (December 26, 1925, *CW*, Vol 29, p. 361). In a tribute reminiscent of the one he had given to Doke more than a decade earlier, Gandhi said of Schreiner:

"She knew no distinction between white and black races. She loved the Indian, the Zulu and the Bantu as her own children. She would prefer to accept the hospitality of a South African Native in his humble hut." (*Idem*).

Gandhi saw clearly the interconnectedness of the various struggles against racial discrimination although he was cautious at this time about the possibility of an amalgamated struggle. Thus in July 1926 Gandhi wrote emphasising a vital axiom about the struggle against racial discrimination which set limits to how far Indian demands could be expected to be met in South Africa without a forward movement in that country as a whole: **"I do not conceive the possibility of justice being done to Indians if none is rendered to natives of the soil". (*Young India*, July 22,**

**1926, *CW*, Vol 31, p. 182)**

Drawing attention, earlier in the same year, to certain racial disabilities in Glasgow in Great Britain, Gandhi made a world-wide projection of his concept of non-violent non-co-operation which he had, six years earlier, introduced in India. Citing the racial disabilities within Britain, he now wrote: "The question therefore that is agitating South Africa is not a local one but it is a tremendous world problem. ...There is however no hope of avoiding the catastrophe unless the spirit of exploitation that at present dominates the nations of the West is transmuted into that of real helpful service, or unless the Asiatic and African races understand that they cannot be exploited without their co-operation, to a large extent voluntary, and thus understanding, withdraw such co-operation". (*Young India*, March 18, 1926, *CW*, Vol 30, pp. 135-136)

The international struggle against race continued to arrest his attention. A mere two months later, Gandhi, writing to Amy Jacques Garvey, acknowledges receipt of books relating to Marcus Garvey. [May 12, 1926, *CW*, Vol 95, (Supplementary Vol V), p. 53]. Miss Garvey wrote: "Of the many acknowledgements of the books received, I cherish most the one from M K Gandhi, the Mahatma of India, dated May 12, 1926, from 'The Ashram, Sabarmati, India.' He addressed me as 'Dear Friend'." [Amy Jacques Garvey, Garvey and Garveyism, Octagon Books, New York, 1986, p. 168, cited in E S Reddy (ed.) *Mahatma Gandhi: Letters to Americans*, Bharatiya Vidya Bhavan, Mumbai, 1998, p.251 and p. 359]

Gandhi had taken France to task for the treatment meted out to the Riffs in Morocco (*Young India*, November 12, 1925, *CW*, Vol 28, p. 441). In an article in *Young India* on October 14, 1926 entitled "Race Arrogance", Gandhi referred to information "showing the wrong done by white Europe to the Abyssinians and the Riffs and the injustice that is being daily perpetrated against the Negro in the United States of America in the name of and for the sake of maintaining white superiority", while reminding Indians that: "Our treatment of the so-called untouchables is no better than that of coloured people by the white man". (*CW*, Vol 31, pp. 492-493)

This is a recurring theme in Gandhi for on January 14, 1926 he had written in *Young India* of the Indian suppressed classes : "We must yield to them the same rights as we would have the Europeans concede to our countrymen in South Africa." (*CW*, Vol 29, p. 400).

"The false and rigid doctrine of inequality has led to the insolent exploitation of the nations of Asia and Africa.", he wrote. (*Young India*, August 11, 1927, *CW*, Vol. 34, p. 315).

A few days later an Indian in Mabuki, in French Africa, wrote to Gandhi about some Indian traders who had lived with Negro women and had offspring but left them behind with no provision for their maintenance. Observing that he had come across similar instances in Delagoa Bay, Gandhi wrote: "The best course, certainly, is that a trader who cannot observe self-control should take his wife with him. If he goes alone and forms a union with a Negro woman, he should behave decently, treat her with love and accept the responsibility of providing for the children which may be born to her. He should understand that under the law, he is bound to provide for the maintenance both of the woman and her children." [(From Gujarati) *Navajivan*, August 28, 1927, *CW*, Vol 34, p. 406]

Some lessons that Gandhi had learnt from African history were to play a profound role in the formulation of his non-cooperation and boycott strategies in India. He had already referred at the end of 1920 to the British evacuation from (the interior of) Somaliland, to suggest that non-cooperation could result in similar withdrawal from India. Eight years later he stressed some economic conclusions not only from the Somali experience but also from the British withdrawal from and subsequent reconquest of the Transvaal. In an article entitled "*How We Lost India*", Gandhi wrote in 1928: "It is characteristic of the British people that they give up their hold on the country from which they can obtain no wealth. They did so in the case of the Transvaal in the year 1884, and when they saw wealth there they launched a war in 1900 in order to gain possession of it. They gave up Somaliland when they could not make money there." [(From Gujarati) *Navajivan*, November 4, 1928, *CW*, Vol 38, p. 14]. British rule, he went on to observe, "functions with the help of our merchants". *(Idem)*. And that was why, Gandhi stresses in the article, boycott of foreign cloth was necessary.

In 1929 Booker T Washington's institute at Tuskegee, Alabama received C F Andrews. After the meeting, Prof Robert Moton, another leading African-American intellectual, who had succeeded Booker T Washington at Tuskegee, sent a message to Gandhi on February 24, 1929: "India, Africa and America joined hands last night. Love and greetings from Tuskegee." (*Young India*, February 28, 1929, *CW*, Vol 40, p. 48) *The Tuskegee Messenger* of March 9, 1929 reported Andrews' message as a "a plain unadorned story of the two greatest spirits in the world today, Tagore and Gandhi." (cited in *Charles Freer Andrews* by Benarsidas Chaturvedi and Marjorie Sykes, first published, London 1949; reprint, Government of India, Publications Division, New Delhi, 1971, pp. 269-270)

Later the same year, Gandhi sent a message, referred to earlier, to *Crisis*, the organ of the National Association for the Advancement of Colored People (NAACP). Its editor, the leading African-American intellectual, Dr W E B DuBois had written to Gandhi requesting a message for the "twelve million people who are the grandchildren of slaves and who amid great difficulties are forging forward in America." [Herbert Aptheker, ed., *The Correspondence of W E B DuBois, Volume* 1, University of Massachusetts Press, (Amherst) 1973, pp 402-403] Gandhi in his message on May 1, 1929 wrote: "Let not the 12 million Negroes be ashamed of the fact that they are the grandchildren of slaves. There is no dishonour in being slaves. There is dishonour in being slave-owners. But let us not think of honour and dishonour in connection with the past."

[See E S Reddy, (ed) *Mahatma Gandhi: Letters to Americans*, op. cit., p 248 and p. 317]

Meanwhile in the South Africa of 1929-30 suggestions would again be made from time to time for adoption of Gandhi's method as, for example, by James Thaele, referred to above, and Brandsby* Ndobe in the Western Cape. According to one account: "At that time Brandsby Ndobe, secretary of the Western Cape ANC, replying to a Court charge of incitement to public violence, explained his speeches as geared to the fight for non-European rights and for equality. He was not, he said, intent on warfare but had always insisted on passive resistance and non-violence; like Thaele, he too used Gandhi as an example." (Walshe, *op. cit.*, p.166)

## VIII

### Prison Again: "our deliverance must mean their deliverance"

In January 1930 *The Cape Times* quoted Dr Abdurrahman, the leader of the Coloured People in South Africa, as telling the Non-European Conference in Cape Town: "You must have a leader who is prepared to make sacrifices, such as Gandhi is in India.... Passive resistance is a weapon that should be properly organised and prepared so that if and when the time comes we shall be ready and could then use it." [Thomas Karis and Gwendolen M. Carter (eds.) *From Protest To Challenge; Volume 1: Protest And Hope 1882-1934* by Sheridan Jones III, Hoover Institution Press, Stanford University, Stanford, 1972, p.268]

In the same year, in March-April 1930, Gandhi led a march to the sea to break the salt law and, having launched Civil Disobedience,

* Sometimes spelt 'Bransby'.

was arrested in May and kept in prison till January 1931.

Helen Joseph, the Englishwoman who was to play an important role in the anti-apartheid struggle in South Africa, was in India between 1928 and 1930. Based then in the relatively quiescent princely state of Hyderabad, she has written about "Gandhi's defiance of the salt tax", which "inspired 100,000 men and women to passive resistance and imprisonment on an unparalleled scale" (Helen Joseph, *Side By Side*, Zed Books, 1986, p. 24).

It was during Gandhi's incarceration that Langston Hughes, who has been described as the poet laureate of African America, penned what was perhaps the first of his many references to Gandhi. Taking Christmas as the peg, Hughes spoke in an ironical tone of imperial gun-boats in China, murder and rape in Africa and also touched this colonial raw nerve:
"Merry Christmas, India, / To Gandhi in his cell, / From righteous Christian England, / Ring out, bright Christmas bell!"
[Merry Christmas, December 1930, Arnold Rampersad & David Roessel (ed.) *The Collected Poems of Langston Hughes*, Vintage Books, New York, 1994, p. 132 and p. 638n]

In the following month, in South Africa, the meeting of the Non-European Conference held in early January 1931 in Bloemfontein, urged steps "toward the total abolition of the pass system since it was regarded as a badge of slavery, failing which (the) Conference would set aside a day not later than during 1934, on which all Africans should destroy their passes." [Leo Kuper, "African Nationalism in South Africa, 1910- 1964" in Monica Wilson & Leonard Thompson (ed.), *The Oxford History of South Africa, Vol II: South Africa 1870-1966*, Oxford, At the Clarendon Press, 1975, p. 446]

Meanwhile in India, a few days later, Gandhi was released from prison in the second half of January 1931.

**On his way to England in September 1931, when Gandhi's**

**ship went through the ports of north-eastern Africa, warm messages of greetings were exchanged between him and Mustafa Nahas Pasha (President of the Wafd party of Egypt), Mohamed Mahmoud Pasha (leader of the Constitutional Liberal Party of Egypt), Safia Zaghloul Pasha (widow of Zaghloul Pasha, the founder of the Wafd) and Cherifa Riaz Pasha ( President of Women's Saadist Committee).[*CW*, Vol 47, pp 400-401 and p. 403]. Gandhi wired Madame Zaghloul Pasha to thank her for her "kind affectionate message". Gandhi remarked on the affectionate nature of the Egyptian messages in a letter written on September 7, 1931 to Jawaharlal Nehru who had stayed back in India (*CW*, Vol 47, p. 402). To the nationalists of Egypt, Gandhi said in a statement given to Al Ahram: "Like us you are an ancient people. I hope you will not slavishly copy all that is Western. If I have understood the events of your country correctly real freedom for Egypt has still to come...." (September 6, 1931, *CW*, Vol 47, p. 397).**

**Gandhi's passage seems to have caught something in the popular imagination in northern Africa, with the renowned Egyptian poet, Ahmad Showquie, composing a long poem of forty verses to mark the event. [Omar El-Haqqaq, Gandhi in Modern Arabic Literature, in B. R Nanda (ed.), *Mahatma Gandhi: 125 Years*, Indian Council of Cultural Relations, New Delhi, 1995, pp 77-79]**

In 1931 British intelligence in Sudan reported: "There is no doubt that especially the younger element of the intelligentsia have a great admiration and sympathy for Gandhi, and that when the movement in India was at its height, they followed the news with keen interest. In private assemblies they discussed the efficiency of the boycott weapon and agreed that Gandhi had discovered in it the only weapon which the...East could employ effectively against imperialism. The influence of Gandhi and Indian politics can be unmistakeably seen in the Gordon College strike (of 1931) and attempted boycott of sugar by pupils". (Based on extract from Political History of Sudan, 1924 to 1931, Archives, Khartoum, reproduced in Muddathir 'Abd Al-Rahim, *Imperialism and Nationalism in the Sudan: A Study in Constitutional and Political Development, 1899-1956*, Clarendon Press, Oxford, 1969, p. 125n)

During his visit to London, Gandhi was asked on October 31, 1931: "For some years Britain would continue certain subject territories like Gold Coast. Would Mr Gandhi object?"

"I would certainly object", was Gandhi's reply (*CW*, Vol 48, p. 255). He continued: "India would certainly aspire after influencing British policy..... I do not want India to be an engine of oppression". (*Idem*) He spoke on this occasion about the exploitation of Zulus and Swazis, which he described as "radically wrong" (*Idem*).

Marcus Garvey had written to Gandhi on behalf of the Universal Negro Improvement Association saying that he was in London for a short while, being due to leave on November 1.

"My people desire me while here to see you", Garvey wrote and suggested October 31 or November 1. (Marcus Garvey to Gandhi, October 29, 1931, *Gandhi Papers*, Vol 52, Serial Number 18198, National Gandhi Museum, New Delhi). Whether a separate meeting could be arranged with Garvey at such short notice is not known, and on the morning of the day of Garvey's departure, Gandhi was scheduled to be in Cambridge.

Speaking there on November 1 at Pembroke College, Gandhi was direct: "What about the South African possession? I would not insist on a transformation of Britain's relations with them, as a condition precedent to our partnership. But I should certainly strive to work for the deliverance of those South African races which, I can say from experience, are ground down under exploitation. Our deliverance must mean their deliverance. But, if that cannot come about, I should have no interest in a partnership with Britain, even if it were of benefit to India. Speaking for myself, I would say that a partnership, giving the promise of a world set free from exploitation, would be a proud privilege for my nation and I would maintain it for ever. But India cannot reconcile herself in any shape or form to any policy of exploitation and, speaking for myself, I may say that, if ever the Congress* should adopt an imperial policy, I should sever my connection with the Congress." (*Young India*, November 19, 1931, *CW*, Vol 48, p. 261)

Ras Makonnen, the Pan-African organiser from British Guiana (now Guyana) in South America, has recorded that during this visit Gandhi "received official treatment" from the League of Coloured Peoples, headed by the Jamaican physician, Dr Harold Moody, and "that was the occasion when Kenyatta first met Gandhi." (Ras Makonnen, *Pan-Africanism From Within*, Oxford University Press, Nairobi, 1973, p. 127) The League had been organised in England by Dr Moody, Jomo Kenyatta and the activist from South India, N G Ranga, who was later prominent in the Indian freedom struggle and peasant movements. (N G Ranga, *Fight For Freedom*, S. Chand & Co, New Delhi, 1968, p.130)

Kenyatta's biographer, Jeremy Murray-Brown, writes about the meeting between Gandhi and the future leader of Kenya:
"Kenyatta met the Indian leader in November 1931, and Gandhi then inscribed Kenyatta's diary with the words: 'Truth and nonviolence can deliver any nation from bondage'. Kenyatta was to give much thought to reconciling that idea with African tradition." (Jeremy Murray-Brown, *Kenyatta*, George Allen & Unwin, London, 1972, pp. 156-157). Kenyatta, who had already been prominent in public activities in Kenya, had contacts with English Quakers with whom Gandhi was in touch. Kenyatta often met Gandhi's friend and biographer C F Andrews at Hampstead. (Murray-Brown, *op. cit.* p.358)

More than twenty years later when the distinguished Indian barrister,

* The reference here is to the Indian National Congress.

Diwan Chaman Lall, would visit Kenyatta in prison as his counsel, he would record: "On the last day of my visit to him , in the small prison at Kepenguria*, he took me into his barn-like cell and bending over his solitary suit-case searched in a corner for a little diary which he had treasured since the year 1931 because it contained an inscription in the hand-writing of Mahatma Gandhi.... A man who cherished Mahatma Gandhi's message of peace and non-violence even within the precincts of the gaol obviously cannot be accused of dictating a different course." [D. Chaman Lall, Foreword to (Indian edition of) Jomo Kenyatta, *Kenya: The Land of Conflict*, The India-Africa Council, New Delhi, 1953, p.1]

**Returning to India in the last week of December 1931, Gandhi was again arrested in the first week of January 1932.**

Africa spoke to him in prison, through Egypt. Messages of sympathy carrying greetings from the Egyptian people came from Safia Zaghloul Pasha and Mustafa Nahas Pasha in September 1932 at the time of Gandhi's fast. From prison Gandhi wired back his thanks to Madame Zaghloul Pasha for a "loving inspiring message" (September 24, 1932, *CW*, Vol 51, p. 133) and to Mustafa Nahas Pasha, "deeply touched" (September 26, 1932, *CW*, Vol 51, p. 142).

Gandhi's thoughts were again on the educational aspects of the struggle against social oppression. While still in Yeravda Central Prison, Gandhi wrote to G. Ramachandra Rao on April 14, 1933 appreciatively of the educational work at the Tuskegee Institute: "I wish you every success in producing an Indian Tuskegee." He asked Rao to devote himself "might and main" to producing, from among the oppressed castes or outcastes, "a prototype of Booker T Washington." (*CW*, Vol 54, p. 406).

Writing a few weeks after his release from prison in May 1933,

* Kapenguria.

Gandhi again commended the work done for Blacks in the United States by the Hampton Institute, Virginia and Tuskegee Institute, associated with the names of General Samuel Armstrong and Booker T Washington respectively. He praised the work of the "white men" at Hampton, comparing it with the work done by some 'upper caste' Hindus for Dalits, or *Harijan*s, in India. Hampton was for Gandhi a "great enterprise and a noble monument of the industrious and exceedingly well-informed zeal of a handful of white reformers".

He referred to Tuskegee as a "noble edifice" built by Booker T Washington with his "limitless faith and equally limitless application". (*Harijan*, July 29, 1933, *CW*, Vol 55, pp. 322-324) He had been an admirer of both General Armstrong and Booker T Washington from his early days in South Africa. (*Indian Opinion*, September 10, 1903, *CW*, Vol 3, pp 437-440). Coming back to India, he had welcomed the decision of the Hassan Municipality in Karnataka in 1927 to establish an institute for the uplift of scheduled tribes "on the lines of the Tuskegee Institute of Booker T. Washington." (August 3, 1927, *CW*, Vol 34, p. 278) Booker T Washington is praised also in Gandhi's "*Satyagraha in South Africa*" which appeared successively in Gujarati and English in the 1920s. In this book the race situation in the United States is also discussed and the practice of lynching African-Americans, in whose case "the black pigment of their skin constitutes their crime", is criticised. (*CW*, Vol 29, p. 78)

Gandhi sent a message on the centenary of the abolition of slavery for the international celebration that was fixed for July 29, 1933 in Hull, England. This was William Wilberforce's native town. (*CW*, Vol 55, p.317) In his message Gandhi said: "India has much to learn from the heroes of the abolition of slavery for we have slavery based upon supposed religious sanction and more poisonous than its Western fellow." **He compared the abolition of slavery with the abolition of untouchability.** (*CW*, Vol 56, pp 88-90)

On May 7, 1934 Gandhi answered some queries from Carl Murphy, President of the Afro-American Newspapers, Inc., publishers of *The Afro-American*, Baltimore, Gandhi wrote: "Prohibition against other people eating in public restaurants and hotels and prohibition of marriage between coloured people and white people I hold to be a negation of civilisation." [Reproduced on February 7, 1948 by *The Afro-American*, Baltimore, a few days after Gandhi's assassination. For text see E S Reddy, (ed) *Mahatma Gandhi: Letters to Americans*, *op. cit.* p. 278]

Speaking to a delegation of African- Americans, including Dr Howard Thurman, Mrs Sue Thurman and Mr Carrol, the Pastor of Salem, in February 1936, Gandhi advised non-violent non-co-operation against any community indulging in lynchings: "I must not wish ill to these, but neither must I co-operate with them. It may be that ordinarily I depend upon the lynching community for my livelihood. I refuse to co-operate with them, refuse even to touch the food that comes from them, and I refuse to co-operate with my brother Negroes who tolerate the wrong. That is the self-immolation I mean. I have often in my life resorted to the plan." (*Harijan*, March 14, 1936, *CW*, Vol 62, p. 201)

Gandhi had asked them about race relations in the United States: "Is the prejudice against colour growing or dying out?" and "Is the union between Negroes and the whites recognized by law?" (*Ibid*., pp 198-199). Dr Thurman tackled the first question, suggesting that the answer varied from place to place, with white students in the South wishing "to improve upon the attitude of their forbears" but things being somewhat ugly in the industrial centres of the Middle West. (*Ibid*., pp. 198-199) Pastor Carrol said in reply to the second question: "Twenty-five states have laws definitely against these unions…." (*Ibid*., p.199) ). Gandhi concluded on a note of hope: " … it may be through the Negroes that the unadulterated message of non-violence will be delivered to the world." (*Ibid*., p. 202) The meeting ended with Mrs Thurman singing two Afro-American spirituals: "Were you there, when they crucified my Lord" and "We are climbing Jacob's ladder" (*Ibid.*, p. 202n).

In the following year Gandhi sent a message to African-Americans through Dr Channing Tobias, an African-American who called on him on January 10, 1937: **"With right which is on their side and the choice of non-violence as their only weapon, if they will make it such, a bright future is assured." ( *CW*, Vol 64, p. 230)**

To Prof Benjamin Mays, an African-American who was then at Howard University and had called on him, Gandhi stressed some important aspects of non-violent struggle. He saw passive resistance as active resistance. According to him: "Passive resistance is a misnomer for non-violent resistance." (*Harijan,* March 20, 1937, *CW*, Vol 64, p.221) Further, Gandhi told Prof. Mays, non-violent resistance had the merit that it could evoke participation on a wide scale: "The maimed and the blind and the leprous cannot join the army of violence. There is also an age-limit for serving in the army. For a non-violent struggle there is no age-limit; the blind and the maimed and the bed-ridden may serve, and not only men but women also. When the spirit of non-violence pervades the people and actually begins to work, its effect is visible to all." (*Ibid.*, p. 223) Later Prof. Mays became President of Morehouse College in Atlanta where Dr. Martin Luther King, Jr., studied. He was a close friend of Dr. King's father and was to deliver the funeral oration when the son was assassinated.

Gandhi had been giving some thought to the future of the Phoenix Trust, the institution he had left behind in South Africa, not far from Durban. On May 21, 1938, 24 years after leaving South Africa, he wrote to his old friend Hermann Kallenbach, "the only active trustee", thinking aloud about the sale of its printing press and still nursing one wish: "I hope we can hold on to the land, turn it into a model agricultural farm, and settle on it Indians or even Zulus – provided of course that is made self-supporting". [*CW*, Vol 96, (Supplementary Vol VI) p 293]

Meanwhile, Italy's role in Abyssinia kept inviting attention. Gandhi's concern for the Abyssinians was reiterated in December 1939 (*Harijan,* December 9, 1939, *CW*, Vol 71, p. 10). As we have seen, Gandhi had already referred to European wrong in Abyssinia (Ethiopia) in *Young India* on October 14, 1926 (*CW*, Vol 31, pp 492). He disapproved of Italy's conduct in relation to Abyssinia, saying in 1935 that it sought "submission of the people of the beautiful land". (*Harijan*, October 10, 1935, *CW*, Vol 62, p. 29)

In 1939 Neville Chamberlain claimed on behalf of the England of his day: "If imperialism means the assertion of racial superiority, suppression of political and economic freedom of other peoples, the exploitation of the resources of other countries for the benefit of an imperialist country, then I say these are not the characteristics of this country." Gandhi answered: "This is pleasing to the ear but does not square with the facts. The policy adopted in Kenya, the clove business in Zanzibar, the Ottawa Pact, not to speak of the Dominions which exploit the so-called uncivilised races of the earth, do not show as if the imperial spirit was dead." (*Harijan*, December 9, 1939, *CW*, Vol 71, p. 6)

## IX

### Prisoner's Call for Freedom for "subject peoples in Asia and Africa": "the only effective means..."

1940 marks the beginning of a politically stressful period in India. Even so, Gandhi not only kept his ear on African affairs but seemed also to be tuning in closely. The South African Constitution came in for severe criticism from Gandhi on September 29, 1940:
"The coloured man is dirt. There shall be no equality between the whites and the coloured races. Thus runs the South African

constitution." (*Harijan*, October 6, 1940, *CW*, Vol 73, p. 65)

There were continual visits and messages to Gandhi from African-Americans. Early in 1942 messages were brought to him from Dr George Washington Carver, the famous Professor of Botany and agricultural scientist at Tuskegee in the United States, with whom Gandhi had been in contact. Carver had been referred to in *Indian Opinion* as early as in February 1909. Langston Hughes, the leading African American writer who wrote a moving poem at the time of Gandhi's fast in prison in February 1943, tells us that like Booker T Washington, "Carver had been born in slavery." (Langston Hughes, *Famous American Negroes*, Dodd, Mead & Company, New York, 1954, p. 69) Carver was about five years elder to Gandhi.

*Harijan* carried the following record of Gandhi's conversation with Dr Carver's representative, Dr John. It suggests that there were earlier contacts between Gandhi and Dr Carver.

"Gandhiji laughingly said: I will not accept the messages, unless Dr Carver comes and delivers them himself.

Dr John said Dr Carver was too old now to come to India. But he remembers Gandhiji whenever he has an Indian visitor...

The very first question that Gandhiji asked Dr John about Dr Carver was: But even this genius suffers under the handicap of segregation, does not he?

Oh yes, as much as any Negro.

And yet these people talk of democracy and equality! It is an utter lie.

But Dr Carver is never bitter or resentful.

I know, that is what we believers in non-violence have to learn from him. But what about the claim of these people who are said to be fighting for democracy?" (*Harijan*, February 15, 1942, CW, Vol 75, p. 292)

When Dr Carver passed away the following year Gandhi was in jail.

A few months before the All India Congress Committee (AICC) of the Indian National Congress decided in 1942 upon the Quit India movement against British rule, Gandhi wrote an article entitled "*To Every Briton*". In it he asked every Briton "to support me in my appeal to the British at this very hour to retire from every Asiatic and African possession and at least from India. That step is necessary for the destruction of Nazism and Fascism. In this I include Japan's 'ism' also. It is a good copy of the two." The article bore the date May 11, 1942, the day after the anniversary of the Great Indian Revolt of 1857, and was published in *Harijan* on May 17, 1942. (*CW*, Vol 76, p. 98)

During this week Gandhi was reported to have told Congressmen: "Even before the communists ever said it, I have been thinking of a new mode of life. But it is impossible unless Britain withdraws to let the Indians and the Negroes be free." (May 15, 1942, CW, Vol 76, p.111) He replied to a cable from "*The Sunday Despatch*" and wired repeating words he had earlier used in an interview to the Press on May 16: "Both America and Britain lack the moral basis for engaging in this war unless they put their own houses in order by making it their fixed determination to withdraw their influence and power both from Africa and Asia and removed the colour bar." (*Harijan*, June 7, 1942, *CW*, Vol 76, p. 164).

At the beginning of the following month Gandhi addressed President Franklin Roosevelt of the United States. A crisis had been building up in India and Gandhi had been thinking in terms of another round of struggle. Even at this time, when Gandhi needed American sympathy, he did not fail pointedly to remind Roosevelt of Africa and of the African-American plight: "I venture to think that the Allied declaration that the Allies are fighting to make the world safe for freedom of the individual and for democracy sounds hollow so long as India and, for that matter, Africa are exploited by Great Britain and America has the Negro problem in her own home. But in order to avoid all complications, in my proposal I have confined myself only to India. If India becomes free, the rest must follow, if it does not happen simultaneously." (July 1, 1942, *CW*, Vol 76, p. 265)

A few days later he noted the Herculean effort made by England to defend itself in the Second World War and wrote: "In their schools the rulers teach us to sing 'Britons never shall be slaves'. How can the refrain enthuse their slaves? The British are pouring blood like water and squandering gold like dust in order to preserve their liberty. Or, is it their right to enslave India and Africa? Why should Indians do less to free themselves from bondage?" (*Harijan*, July 12, 1942, *CW*, Vol 76, p. 273)

A fortnight later another article by Gandhi, dated July 18, 1942, under the title "*To Every Japanese*" was carried in the *Harijan*. **Gandhi wrote: "Even if you win it will not prove that you were in the right; it will only prove that your power of destruction was greater. This applies obviously to the Allies too, unless they perform *now* the just and righteous act of freeing India as an earnest and promise of similarly freeing all other subject peoples in Asia and Africa." (*Harijan*, July 26, 1942, *CW*, Vol 76, p. 311) He was to be arrested within the subsequent 15 days upon the adoption of the famous Quit India Resolution by the All India Congress Committee at its Bombay session on August 8, 1942.**

**Langston Hughes summed up both the African-American and Gandhi's case:**

**"If you believe/ In the Four Freedoms, too. / Then share 'em with me – / Don't keep 'em all for you / ..... You can't lock up Gandhi, / Club Roland Hayes, / Then make fine speeches / About Freedom's ways."** [How About It, Dixie, October 1942, in Arnold

Rampersad & David Roessel (ed.) *op. cit.*, p.291 and p.659n]*

In September 1942, the African-American leader and trade-unionist, A Philip Randolph, had addressed a Conference of the March-on-Washington Movement in Detroit, United States. Randolph, who had become known for organising a national union of Sleeping Car Workers in 1925, had given a call in 1941 for a march by thousands of African-Americans to demand employment opportunities. In response, US President Franklin Roosevelt had issued an order establishing the Fair Employment Practices Committee. Randolph had then called off the march but the Movement to which the call gave birth remained. At the Detroit Conference, Randolph "suggested affinities between the Movement's technique of mass action and Gandhi's nonviolent direct action in India." [Francis L. Broderick and August Meier, (ed.) *Negro Protest Thought in the Twentieth Century*, The Bobbs-Merrill Company, Indianapolis, 1965, p. 201]

Calling for the building up of organisational capacity to wage mass struggle, Randolph said: "Witness the strategy and maneuver of the people of India with mass civil disobedience and non-co-operation and the marches to the sea to make salt. It may be said that the Indian people have not won their freedom. This is so but they will win it." (*Ibid.*, p. 207) He declared: "India is now waging a world shaking, history making fight for independence. India's fight is the Negro's fight." ( *Ibid.*, 210)

There was to be no thoughtless borrowing though. In March 1943 Dr W E B DuBois, who admired Gandhi, discussed in an article the possibilities of non-violent non-co-operation being adopted by African-Americans but pointed to certain differences between the

---

*A similar spirit of requiring that the proposed rights and freedoms be universally applied is reflected in the ANC document "Africans' Claims in South Africa" drawn up and adopted at the annual conference of the ANC at Bloemfontein on December 16, 1943. This is considered one of the most important documents of the ANC and was drafted by a committee headed by Professor Z. K. Matthews. It was published with a preface by Dr A. B. Xuma, President-General of the ANC. The document contains an analysis of the Atlantic Charter of 1941 from an African point of view and has been described as a Bill of Rights.

Indian situation and that prevailing in America. He stressed that "insofar as this partakes of the nature of a general strike, we must remember that while the Indians form practically the whole working class of India, without whose co-operation all industry would collapse, American Negroes are but a fifteenth or at most a tenth and can be and indeed often are, replaced and barred from work". [W E B DuBois, Doubts Gandhi Plan, *Amsterdam News*, March 13, 1943, in David Levering Lewis (ed.), *W E B DuBois: A Reader*, Henry Holt & Company, New York, 1995, p 409 ]

The problem in America was to expand work opportunities for the African-Americans and Dr DuBois did not therefore recommend strikes. The weapons and tactics in the two situations could not be the same. He felt also that "we…are not ready for systematic lawbreaking" and doubted whether this was "good policy" in the American context. (*Idem*) Dr DuBois made a reference to Gandhi's fast in jail, a few days earlier in February-March 1943, which "is setting four hundred millions of men aquiver and may yet rock the world" while suggesting that such methods would probably not work in the West. (*Idem*)

**A couple of years later Dr DuBois was to preside over the Pan-African Congress which recommended the Gandhian method of non-violent non-co-operation for Africa.**

**The poet did not miss the significance of Gandhi's February-March 1943 fast in prison; Langston Hughes' message to Britain is sent out through the Baltimore Afro-American even as the fast is on: All of Asia's watching/ And I'm watching, too, / For I am also jim crowed —/ As India is jim crowed by you.** ["Ghandhi (sic) is Fasting", February 20, 1943, in Arnold Rampersad & David Roessel (ed.) *op. cit.*, p.578 and p.693n]

**The spectacle of Gandhi's struggle in India during the war years was a factor that probably added to the growing impatience for change among young Africans in South Africa. (See Jordan**

**K. Ngubane, *An African Explains Apartheid*: Frederick A. Praeger Publishers, New York, 1963, p. 96 and Mary Benson, *The African Patriots: The Story of the African National Congress of South Africa*, Faber & Faber, London, 1963, p. 109)**

**While under detention, Gandhi wrote to the Government on July 15, 1943. In his letter, Gandhi reproduced the passage from his article in the *Harijan* dated July 26, 1942 seeking the freeing of "all other subject peoples in Asia and Africa". Indeed, he described a long quotation from the article, including this passage, as "an open gate to the whole of my mind regarding the movement contemplated in the resolution of 8th August last." (Letter to Additional Secretary, Home Department, Government of India, July 15, 1943, *CW*, Vol 77, pp 128-129)**

This sequence of events came to be known in Africa. More than a decade later, on June 11, 1957, Nigeria's leader, **Dr Nnamdi Azikiwe**, speaking at Oxford, reminded his audience that in the 1940s the Labour opposition in the British House of Commons had pressed Mr Amery, the Secretary of State for India, to release Mahatma Gandhi and Jawaharlal Nehru from prison. Dr Azikiwe observed: "Mr Amery prevaricated, and on being requested to state categorically what India wanted, Mahatma Gandhi said that Indian nationalists demanded from Britain self-government for India and for the people of Africa." (*Zik: A Selection From the Speeches of Nnamdi Azikiwe, Governor General of the Federation of Nigeria*, Cambridge University Press, London, 1961, pp. 315-316)

The Indian peasant movement leader, N G Ranga, interviewed Gandhi on October 29, 1944 a few months after the latter's release from detention. Ranga asked him: "Are we right in thinking that your stand against world imperialism is intended to benefit as much the African, Chinese, Red Indians and other non-white masses as the 400 millions of India?" Gandhi replied: "My correspondence with the Government while under detention shows that most clearly." (*CW*, Vol 78, p. 251) Ranga went on to inform Gandhi that "several of our friends and your admirers in England, Africa and the West Indies, such as Mr Reginald Reynolds, Miss Stock Kenyatta, Mr George Padmore, have already been working on your lines for the emancipation of the colonial and coloured peoples." (*Idem*)*

The International African Service Bureau, established in the 1930s by Padmore and others, had been merged into the Pan-African Federation. Padmore tells us: "Theoretical problems such as the methods and forms of organisation to be adopted by colonial peoples; the tactics and strategy of the national freedom struggle; the applicability of Gandhian non-violent non-co-operating techniques to the African situation were all openly discussed and debated in the columns of the Federation's journal, *International African Opinion*, edited by the distinguished West Indian historian, C L R James and assisted by William Harrison, an erudite Afro-American Harvard scholar ..." (George Padmore, *Pan-Africanism or Communism*?, Dobson, London, 1956, p. 130)

In the United States, A Philip Randolph reasserted the interconnectedness of the struggle: "The March on Washington movement proclaims the slogan of a free Africa. It joins the cry of a 'Fight for a Free India and China'. " [A Philip Randolph in Rayford W. Logan (ed.), *What the Negro Wants*, The University of North Carolina Press, Chapel Hill, 1944, p. 134]. Of the Second World War, Randolph wrote: "But this war need not be a world movement of reaction . The people can make it a Peoples' Revolution – a

* There is perhaps an error here mainly in the form of a missing comma after the name of Ms Stock. Ranga, who had spent many years in England, had worked closely with both Jomo Kenyatta and the Englishwoman, Ms Dinah Stock. Ranga writes of the latter: "After Jomo Kenyatta and I had founded the League of Coloured Peoples in 1930-31, she aided him ably in his work in England for Kenya's freedom. When I wanted to form the Colonial and Coloured Peoples' Freedom Front in 1944 with the blessings of Mahatma Gandhi and sought her co-operation, she readily responded." (N G Ranga, *Fight For Freedom*, op. cit., p. 92; see also Ras Makonnen, *op. cit.*, p. 191)

Revolution whose dynamism against Axis tyranny will be greater and more powerful because it will possess the fighting faith and crusading confidence of the masses of all colors and races. The people can cause this war to usher in the Century of the Common Man. This is the meaning of the call of Gandhi for an independent and free India. It is the reason for the stirrings of the 'natives' of Africa, the war by the Chinese against the dominion of Nippon, the rebellion of the blacks in the Caribbean Islands against a bare subsistence wage, and the fight of the Negro people of the United States for equality." (*Ibid.*, p. 135) Writing during the war years of the forties, Mary McLeod Bethune, President of the National Council of Negro Women, and Leslie Pinckney Hill, who had taught at Tuskegee Institute from 1904 to 1907, could see from an Afro-American perspective either some connection with or an inspiration in Gandhi. [Logan (ed.), *op. cit.* p. 252 and p. 75]

Around this time the leading African-American historian, Carter G. Woodson, wrote appreciatively of the struggle that Gandhi had led in South Africa "fearlessly fighting disabilities imposed...by the Asiatic Law Amendment Act of 1907." (Carter Godwin Woodson, *African Heroes and Heroines*, The Associated Publishers, Washington, Second Edition, 1944, p.153)

At the beginning of 1945, Dr W E B DuBois criticised the British colonial tendency repeatedly to detain leaders like Mahatma Gandhi, Sarojini Naidu , Jawaharlal Nehru and Dr Syed Mahmud. (W E B DuBois, *Color and Democracy: Colonies and Peace*, Harcourt, Brace and Company, New York, 1945, p. 32)

Meanwhile, as the Second World War had drawn to a close, the Allies turned their attention to the emerging world order.

At the time of the San Francisco conference which convened on April 25, 1945, leading up to the formation of the United Nations, Gandhi issued a statement in which he warned that "there will be no peace for the Allies or the world unless they shed their belief in the efficacy of war and its accompanying terrible deception and fraud and are determined to hammer out real peace based on freedom and equality of all races and nations." (*The Bombay Chronicle*, April 18, 1945, *CW*, Vol 79, p. 389)

Gandhi's message to the San Francisco conference was repeated to Denton J. Brooks Jr, a Black journalist from America who met Gandhi around May 30, 1945. To him Gandhi said the memorable words: "My life is its own message." (*The Hindu*, June 15, 1945, *CW*, Vol 80, p. 209)

Around June 13, 1945 Gandhi sent a cable to the British Labour leader Fenner Brockway in which the opening sentence was pithy: "Indian freedom campaign is for the world's Asiatic, Negro and other exploited races' freedom." (*The Hindu*, June 15, 1945, *CW*, Vol 80, p. 311)

Later in 1945 another Pan-African Congress — variously described as the Fifth or the Sixth depending upon whether an early conference held in 1900 at the initiative of Henry Sylvester Williams is to be counted or not — was held in Manchester, England between October 15-21, 1945 under inspiration from **Dr DuBois who was also personally present. George Padmore,** the Trinidad-born activist, and **Kwame Nkrumah**, the future leader of Ghana, were the leading organisers. **At the conference, the *satyagraha* methods of Mahatma Gandhi "had been discussed and ... endorsed as the only effective means of making alien rulers respect the wishes of an unarmed subject people ." (George Padmore, *Pan-Africanism or Communism?, op. cit.*, p. 177)**

As Nkrumah later recorded of the proceedings at Manchester: **"A definite programme of action was agreed upon. Basically, the programme centred around the demand for constitutional change, providing for universal suffrage. The methods to be employed were based on the Gandhist technique of non-violent non-co-operation, in other words, the withholding of labour,**

**civil disobedience and economic boycott."** (Kwame Nkrumah, *Africa Must Unite*, Heinemann Educational Books, London, 1963, pp 134-5).

Kenyatta, who had met Gandhi in 1931, was also present at this meeting as Chairman of the Credentials Committee, as was "Sierra Leone's redoubtable trade union leader, Wallace Johnson". (Colin Legum, *Pan-Africanism: A Short Political Guide*, Frederick A. Praeger, New York, 1962, p. 31) **From South Africa the ANC named Marko Hlubi, already in England, to the Pan-African Congress. " He and the other South African delegate, Peter Abrahams, the writer, met many of Africa's young leaders, among them Kwame Nkrumah, Chief Akintola ...." (Mary Benson, *The African Patriots: The Story of the African National Congress of South Africa*, Faber & Faber, London, 1963, p. 117)** The Congress set up a working committee with Dr DuBois as Chairman and Nkrumah as secretary.

## X

### Endorsement of Joint Struggle in South Africa: "... he had inspired us deeply...."

As the British endgame in India started in 1945, one of Gandhi's most important political interviews was given in Shimla to an African-American journalist, Frank E. Bolden, who met him as "a representative of the combined Coloured press of America". The interview which was scheduled to be a short one, actually went on to more than two hours. It was published in *The Afro-American*, Baltimore on August 18, 1945.

The well known folk music promoter, Harold Leventhal, who was posted in India during the Second World War with the US Army

Signal Corps, came to know Jawaharlal Nehru and through him secured an audience with Gandhi. Later, in 1998, Leventhal was to write in *The New York Times*: " The first thing he (Gandhi) wanted to know was how Paul Robeson was." (See Margalit Fox in *New York Times*, October 6, 2005, reproduced as "Harold Leventhal Is No More", in *Mainstream,* New Delhi, October 15, 2005). Robeson, who graduated as a lawyer but made a name on the stage and in music, was a friend and disciple of Dr DuBois. Gandhi, who had met Robeson's wife in London in 1931, knew of Robeson as a fighter against racism and colonialism.

Troops from West Africa were utilized by Britain in the South East Asian theatre. The came into contact with "politically minded Asiatics reaching out towards political independence" (I. Wallerstein, *The Road to Independence: Ghana and the Ivory Coast,* Mouton & Co., Paris, 1964, p. 79n) Black soldiers from West Africa also met Gandhi in Madras (now Chennai) in early 1946. They asked him: "How can a continent like Africa fight down the fetters of slavery when it is so hopelessly divided?" His advice was the simple message he had been infusing in India since 1920: "But there is a charm which can overcome all these handicaps. The moment the slave resolves that he will no longer be a slave, his fetters fall. He frees himself and shows the way to others." (*Harijan,* February 24, 1946, *CW*, Vol 83, p. 11) They asked further: " Africa and India both drink of the cup of slavery. What necessary steps can be taken to unite the two nations so as to present a common front?" He replied: "You are right. India is not yet free and yet Indians have begun to realize that their freedom is coming, not because the white man says so but because they have developed the power within. Inasmuch as India's struggle is non-violent, it is a struggle for the emancipation of all oppressed races against superior might. I do not propose mechanical joint action between them. 'Each one has to find his own salvation' is true of this as well as the other world. It is enough that there is a real moral bond between Asiatics and Africans. It will grow as time passes." (*Ibid.*, p. 12) He told them that he wanted Indo-African trade to be non-exploitative and "not of manufactured goods against raw materials after the fashion of Western exploiters".

A noteworthy observation that he made to the West African soldiers was about the spinning wheel which he had popularised in India as part of his programme for reconstruction and utilisation of idle labour time and thereby end widespread poverty: "If I had discovered it in South Africa, I would have introduced it among the Africans who were my neighbours in Phoenix. You can grow cotton, you have ample leisure and plenty of manual skill. You should study and adopt the lesson of the village crafts we are trying to revive. Therein lies the key to your salvation." (*Ibid.* p. 13)

A deputation of South African Indians met Gandhi in March 1946. In the Memorandum for the Viceroy that he drafted for possible use by them, Gandhi made reference to the formation of the Union of South Africa in the early years of the century and wrote: "One would have thought that the advent of Union would mean the union of all the races of South Africa, ie the African (the Negro), the European, and the Asiatics (primarily and principally Indians). What a noble tradition such a Union would have been for the world. But it was not to be. On the contrary, the Union became an anti-African and anti-Asiatic combine." (*CW*, Vol 83, p. 231) Of the proposed Land and Franchise Bill, which had brought the delegation to India, Gandhi wrote: "though superficially it affects the Indians of Natal and the Transvaal (it) is in effect a challenge to Asia and by implication to the Negro races." (*Harijan*, March 24, 1946, *CW*, Vol 83, p. 284)

In mid-June 1946 the Indian community began passive resistance in South Africa. Seeing the struggle on a broad canvas, Gandhi wrote on June 26, 1946: "The real 'white man's burden' is not insolently to dominate coloured or black people under the guise of protection; it is to desist from the hypocrisy which is eating into them. It is time white men learnt to treat every human being as their equal. There is no mystery about whiteness of the skin. It has repeatedly been proved that given equal opportunity a man, be he of any colour or country, is fully equal to any other." (*Harijan*, June 30, 1946, *CW*, Vol 84, p. 372) He continued: "Is a civilisation worth the name which requires for its existence the very doubtful prop of racial legislation and lynch law?" (*Ibid*, p. 373)

A rather moving re-affirmation of Gandhi's African commitment is pointed to by E S Reddy, a friend of several South African leaders and especially of Oliver Tambo who was President of the ANC in its years of decisive struggle. Reddy observes: "I might also recall that in 1946 when white gangsters were brutally attacking Indian passive resisters in Durban, Gandhiji told the All India Congress Committee that he would not shed a single tear if all the Indian satyagrahis were wiped out, for they would thereby point the way to the Africans and vindicate the honour of India." (E S Reddy, *Gandhiji's Vision of a Free South Africa, op. cit.* p 140; see also p.116) The meeting Reddy refers to took place in Bombay on July 7, 1946. These are Gandhi's entire words: "The land in South Africa does not belong to the whites. Land belongs to one who labours on it. I would not shed a single tear if all the satyagrahis in South Africa are wiped out. Thereby they will not only bring deliverance to themselves but point the way to the Negroes and vindicate the honour of India". (*CW* Vol 84, p 422) Gandhi concluded, characteristically turning the gaze inward, to the treatment given to a section of the society in India: "We turned a portion of ourselves into pariahs and today the whites of South Africa are doing the same to our compatriots there. Let us purge ourselves of this curse and bless the heroic struggle of our brethren in South Africa." (*Idem*)

Independent India's boycott of apartheid South Africa was in one sense presaged before independence by Gandhi himself. Private institutions in India responded in their own way to the ongoing Indian struggle in South Africa. The Taj Mahal Hotel in Bombay had put up a notice: "South Africans not admitted." The American journalist, Louis Fischer interviewed Gandhi on July 17, 1946. Among the many things they discussed was the Taj Mahal Hotel's policy. Fischer disapproved of the notice, saying "I do not like it. Your non-violence should be more generous." Gandhi replied: "That won't be non-violence. Today the white man rules in India. So if the Taj Mahal has the gumption to put up that notice, it is a feather in its cap." (*Harijan*, August 4, 1946, *CW*, Vol 85, p. 10)

Meanwhile, Gandhi had been corresponding with the Governor-General of Portuguese India, concerning the state of civil liberties in Goa. Writing to him on August 2, 1946, Gandhi recalled his experience of Portuguese-ruled Africa: "I suppose you know that I have visited Mozambique, Delagoa and Inhambane. I did not notice there any government for philanthropic purposes. Indeed, I was astonished to see the distinction that the Government made between Indians and the Portuguese and between the Africans and themselves." (*Harijan*, August 11, 1946, *CW*, Vol 85, pp 109-110)

Inter-communal relations within India had worsened and Gandhi was trying to bring peace in the Noakhali area in East Bengal when Professor Stuart Nelson of Howard University, Washington, joined him in prayer. At a prayer meeting in Srirampur on December 3, 1946, the African-American recited from Isaac Watt's hymn "Our God, our help in ages past." (*Harijan*, January 5, 1947, *CW* Vol 86, p. 187) Gandhi, who translated the meaning of the hymn for his audience, recorded that "we immediately became as old friends." (Letter dated December 4, 1946 to E Stanley Jones, *CW*, Vol 94, p. 313)

Around this time African leaders like Bildad Kaggia, in Kenya, and Kenneth Kaunda, in the then Northern Rhodesia, had started their own organisational activities. Subsequently, in the course of his trial in the 1950s, Kaggia was to cite Gandhi as his inspiration. (Montagu Slater, *The Trial of Jomo Kenyatta*, Secker & Warburg,

London, 1955, p. 194) The writer Fergus Macpherson records a conversation in early 1947 with Kaunda, then in his mid-twenties, who was later to be President of Zambia: "The 'nonviolent positive action' of Mahatma Gandhi, he said, was perhaps the answer…." (Fergus Macpherson, *Kenneth Kaunda of Zambia : The Times and the Man*, Oxford University Press, Lusaka, 1974, p. 70) Later the British Socialist Fenner Brockway would refer to Kaunda as "the African Gandhi". (Fenner Brockway, *Outside the Right*, George Allen & Unwin, London, 1963, p. 158)

A variety of key figures were similarly affected or influenced. Gandhi's work was being followed with interest by diverse groups in other parts of Africa as well. In France-dominated Africa, for example, Tunisia's Habib Bourguiba, who has been described as one of North Africa's most creative leaders, became a close observer of Gandhi's ideas and methods and believed like him that the struggle against colonialism was essentially the task of recovering the power of independent thinking and that the main thing was to rid the colonised mind of its servility. (Felix Garas, Bourguiba: *La Naissance d'une Nation*, Rene Julliard, Paris, 1956, pp. 9–11 and pp. 65-67)

**Meanwhile, the struggle in South Africa continued to occupy Gandhi's attention. He was still on his peace mission in East Bengal when on February 28, 1947 he endorsed the decision of the African National Congress, the Coloured People's Organisation , the Natal Indian Congress and the Transvaal Indian Congress in South Africa to refrain from assisting the celebrations of and to boycott a Royal visit to that country "in view of the disabilities imposed upon the Asiatics and Africans and other Coloured people". He wrote: "I take this opportunity of publicly endorsing the abstention as a natural and dignified step by any self-respecting body of people." (*The Hindu*, March 1, 1947, *CW*, Vol 87, p. 28)**

**Within ten days of this endorsement followed the famous**

**Doctors' Pact, on March 9, 1947, in which "Dr Xuma for the ANC, joined with Dr Naicker and Dr Dadoo the Presidents of the Natal and Transvaal Indian Congresses, in signing this agreement to work for full franchise rights and for equal economic and industrial rights and opportunities as well as other freedoms." (Mary Benson, *The African Patriots, op. cit.* p. 140)**

**"Three days later", continues Benson, "Naicker and Dadoo flew to India to attend the first Inter-Asian Conference, carrying with them the good wishes of many meetings of Africans and Indians – including a message from Anton Lembede." (*Idem*) Lembede was leader of the ANC Youth League. A new generation in South Africa was coming into its own.**

**Responding on May 5, 1947 to a cable from Yusuf Cachalia, the Honorary Secretary of the Transvaal Indian Congress in the context of increasing efforts for a joint struggle with "inclusion of all the races", Gandhi agreed that this was "logically correct" but underlined his concern that the highest standards of non-violence be maintained. (*CW*, Vol 87, p. 414)**

On the morning of May 18, 1947, Gandhi, wrote out a message to South Africa which he sent through Dr Yusuf Dadoo and Dr G. M. Naicker, then visiting India. The two had come over to Patna to meet him again after having seen him earlier in Delhi. Gandhi wrote: "To the people of South Africa, to whom I am no stranger, I would say that they should not make the position of their representatives impossible by their unwarranted prejudice against colour. The future is surely not with the so-called white races if they keep themselves in purdah. The attitude of unreason will mean a third war which sane people should avoid. Political co-operation among all the exploited races in South Africa can only result in mutual goodwill, if it is wisely directed and based on truth and non-violence." (*Harijan*, May 25, 1947, *CW*, Vol 87, p. 492; see also p. 495)

As noticed in the Overview in Section I above, there were to be debates within the African National Congress on the subject of non-violence which in some way paralleled the debates in the Indian National Congress on the same issue particularly in 1934. Though the freedom movements in India and in Africa sought out their own answers to the question, the fact of the debate ensured an element of deliberation which earned a measure of universal respect for both liberation movements.

**Less than nine months after his message to the people of South Africa, Gandhi was shot dead in January 1948. "We too mourned his death", wrote Kwame Nkrumah, "for he had inspired us deeply with his political thought, notably with his adherence to non-violent resistance." (Kwame Nkrumah, *I Speak of Freedom: A Statement of African Ideology*, Heinemann, London, 1961, pp 2-3)**

When, in April 1994, 46 years after Gandhi's assassination, Nelson Mandela cast his vote in a resurgent South Africa, he chose to do so in Inanda, where Gandhi's friend John Dube lay buried. Mandela wrote: "I voted at Ohlange High School in Inanda, a green and hilly township just north of Durban, for it was there that John Dube, the first President of the ANC, was buried. This African patriot had helped found the organisation in 1912, and casting my vote near his graveside brought history full circle, for the mission he began eighty-two years before was about to be achieved." (Nelson Mandela, *Long Walk To Freedom*, Abacus edition, Little, Brown & Company, London, 1999, p. 742)

# XI

## Epilogue: "go to prison for their beliefs as Gandhi had"

This essay has not focussed on the *Indian* struggle in South Africa, several accounts of which are available, including Gandhi's own *Satyagraha In South Africa*. Later, as a South Africa–born Indian generation came into its own, this struggle coalesced into the larger South African struggle.

An attempt has been made here to explore some of the live intersections between the African struggles and Gandhi during his lifetime, particularly since his fuller political evolution that had taken place by the high noon of his South African phase. The attempt has been also to bring together some references on the subject so that they may furnish openings for further research.

Though we have not told the story of the early Indian struggle in South Africa here, there is one aspect of it – its power of example - that perhaps merits some emphasis even in this essay.

Referring to the 1946-48 movement in South Africa and Gandhi's contact with it, E S Reddy has written: "In a sense his last Satyagraha was also in South Africa. Though he could not be physically present, he guided and inspired the great Indian passive resistance movement of 1946-48 and lent it enormous support." (E S Reddy, "*Gandhiji*", article dated January 30, 1988, in *Gandhi, Nehru and Freedom Struggle In South Africa*, A Mainstream Publication, New Delhi, n.d., p.1)

**Of this "last Satyagraha", in which some Coloured people, whites and Africans actually went to prison in solidarity with the Indians, Nelson Mandela has given us the following account**: *"That same year, another event forced me to recast my whole approach to political work. In 1946, the Smuts government passed* *the Asiatic Land Tenure Act, which curtailed the free movement of Indians, circumscribed the areas where Indians could reside and trade, and severely restricted their right to buy property. In return, they were provided with representation in Parliament by token white surrogates. Dr Dadoo, president of the Transvaal Indian Congress, castigated the restrictions and dismissed the offer of parliamentary representation as 'a spurious offer of a sham franchise'. This law – known as the Ghetto Act – was a grave insult to the Indian community and anticipated the Group Areas Act, which would eventually circumscribe the freedom of all South Africans of colour.*

*The Indian community was outraged and launched a concerted two-year campaign of passive resistance to oppose the measures. Led by Dr Dadoo and Dr G .M. Naicker, president of the Natal Indian Congress (NIC), the Indian community conducted a mass campaign that impressed us with its organization and dedication. Housewives, priests, doctors, lawyers, traders, students and workers took their place in the front lines of the protest. For two years, people suspended their lives to take up the battle. Mass rallies were held; land reserved for whites was occupied and picketed. No fewer than 2,000 volunteers went to jail, and Dr Dadoo and Dr Naicker were sentenced to six months' hard labour.*

*The campaign was confined to the Indian community, and the participation of other groups was not encouraged. Even so, Dr Xuma and other African leaders spoke at several meetings, and along with the Youth League gave full moral support to the struggle of the Indian people. The government crippled the rebellion with harsh laws and intimidation, but we in the Youth League and the ANC had witnessed the Indian people register an extraordinary protest against colour oppression in a way that Africans and the ANC had not.*

*Ismail Meer and J.N. Singh suspended their studies, said good-bye to their families and went to prison. Ahmed Kathrada, who was still a high-school student, did the same thing.... If I had once questioned the willingness of the Indian community to protest against oppression, I no longer could.*

*The Indian campaign became a model for the type of protest that we in the Youth League were calling for.*

*It instilled a spirit of defiance and radicalism among the people, broke the fear of prison, and boosted the popularity and influence of the NIC and TIC. They reminded us that the freedom struggle was not merely a question of making speeches, holding meetings, passing resolutions and sending deputations, but of meticulous organization, militant mass action and, above all, the willingness to suffer and sacrifice. The Indians' campaign harkened back to the 1913 passive resistance campaign in which Mahatma Gandhi led a tumultuous procession of Indians crossing illegally from Natal to the Transvaal. That was history; this campaign was taking place before my own eyes." (Nelson Mandela, op. cit., pp 118-119).*

An "entire branch of the ANC, from Germiston, joined the resistance in order to show solidarity with an oppressed section of the population and in the belief that in time all Non-European people would unite against common injustice." (Mary Benson, *The African Patriots*, *op. cit*, p. 122) Interestingly, Germiston is where Gandhi had spoken in June 1909 commending the method of passive resistance to the Africans.

According to one account of the events in 1946: "A leading ANC official from Germiston, Joshua Makue and Reverend Michael Scott both participated in the Passive Resistance campaign. The campaigners also lent their support to the mineworkers' strike in the same year, and protested against its ruthless suppression. The outcome was a sense of a common, wider cause." (Elinor Sisulu, *Walter & Albertina Sisulu: In Our Lifetime*, David Philip Publishers, Claremont, South Africa, 2003, p.110)

Makue was a member of a batch led by A.H. Mayes, an European from Germiston. It included three other Africans who joined the resistance and were also imprisoned: Eric Mlangeni, Simon Keitsane and Eric Johannes Nyembe. Makue made a memorable speech in court emphasizing the need " to unite against the common injustice to people of colour in this country." (*Passive Resister*, Johannesburg, October 21, 1946) The passive resistance saw, as Dr. Dadoo was to put it, "active participation and heroic sacrifices" also from prominent Europeans like Rev. Satchell, Mary Barr, Max Itzkin and others. Many from among the Coloured People also participated.

These accounts may provide some insight also on the impact that Gandhi's passive resistance campaign in the Transvaal from 1907 and the wider 1913 campaign may have had on such of his contemporaries in the continent who saw those campaigns unfold in front of them. John Dube's own appreciation for what he then saw was expressed in a talk with Rev W W Pearson in 1914 (See E S Reddy, *Gandhiji's Vision of a Free South Africa, op. cit.*, pp 23-25).

A year after the 1946-48 movement, the ANC annual conference was to take place in Bloemfontein where the Congress Youth League's dynamic Programme of Action was adopted. Mandela writes:

"A few weeks before the conference Walter Sisulu, Oliver Tambo and I met Dr Xuma privately at his home in Sophiatown. We explained that we thought the time had come for mass action along the lines of Gandhi's non-violent protests in India and the 1946 passive resistance campaign ... The ANC's leaders, we said, had to be willing to violate the law and if necessary go to prison for their beliefs as Gandhi had." (Nelson Mandela, op. cit. p. 130)

Other campaigns followed and by a law of progression, as it were, the stage was set for an amalgamated campaign.

Of the successful Campaign of Defiance Against Unjust Laws of

1952, Chief Albert Luthuli, once a student at John Dube's Ohlange institution, and like Mandela a hero of the African struggle, tells us: "The fact that the African and Indian Congresses were participating jointly, and that we were joined by some coloured organisations — the coloured people had no national organisation – limited the scope of what we could jointly defy. Different laws oppress different non-white groups. What we all had in common, however, was the humiliation of discrimination in public places. For this reason the main force of the Defiance Campaign was directed against the national motto of white South Africa, EUROPEANS ONLY, which is found across the length and breadth of the country." (Albert Luthuli, *Let My People Go: An Autobiography*, Collins, London, 1962, p. 117)

"My husband and the ANC", wrote Nokukhanya Luthuli, "were deeply influenced by the non-violent philosophy of Mahatma Gandhi". (Brian Frost, *Struggling to Forgive: Nelson Mandela and South Africa's Search for Reconciliation*, Harper Collins, London, 1998, p. 50 and p. 228n, citing Peter Rule, *Nokukhanya: Mother of Light*, The Grail, South Africa, 1993, p. 56)

The testimony of the ANC leader, M B Yengwa during the Treason Trial in South Africa in the fifties is specific:
"Would you say that the African National Congress as such has taken over the whole philosophy of Gandhi?

No, my Lord, it has not done so.

Do you think Gandhi's ideas have had any influence on African National Congress policy?

It has had a very strong influence on the African National Congress.

In what direction?

In the direction of non-violence my Lord..."

(E S Reddy, *Gandhiji's Vision of a Free South Africa*, op. cit., p. 67, based on Treason Trial Transcript)

Yengwa was a close associate of Albert Luthuli.

As independence dawned in some parts of Africa, repression had mounted in others. The Gold Coast having become the independent state of Ghana in 1957, the All African Peoples' Conference was organised in Accra in 1958. **A posthumously published work by Kwame Nkrumah reproduces the provisional agenda prepared for the conference: "The main purpose of the All-African Peoples' Conference to be held in Accra, Ghana, in December 1958, will be to formulate concrete plans and work out the Gandhian tactics and strategy of the African Non-violent Revolution...." (Kwame Nkrumah, *Revolutionary Path*, International Publishers, New York, 1973, pp 132-133)**

The famous South African writer Ezekiel Mphahlele, who represented the ANC at the Conference, tells us that an Egyptian participant "successfully urged deleting from the provisional agenda the item binding the conference to formulate strategy for the overthrow of colonialism on the basis of Gandhian passive resistance. It was agreed that it was not the responsibility of the conference to impose any method of struggle on any liberatory organization." [Ezekiel Mphahlele, Accra Conference Diary, in *An African Treasury* (selected by Langston Hughes), Victor Gollancz, London, 1961, p. 38]

The Kenyan leader, Tom Mboya, who was at the Conference, records that he "supported the large majority of the delegates who felt strongly that violence as a policy could not work". (Tom Mboya, *Freedom and After*, Andre Deutsch, London, 1963, p. 50) Mboya understood "the importance of mobilization of the entire population" and saw this as "virtually the same tactics" as Gandhi's. *(Ibid*, p. 62) However, he was also of the view that there were limitations to the use of Gandhi's methods in Africa: "The most one can do in the spirit of Gandhi is to follow a course of positive non-violent action—but always with the understanding that it could lead to violence." *(Ibid*, p. 52)

This appeared to be Mphahlele's understanding as well. (See Brian Bunting, *Moses Kotane: South African Revolutionary: A Political Biography*, Inkululeko Publications, London, 1975, p. 242)

Violence was always lurking around the corner. In a pamphlet first written and circulated in the forties, Nkrumah, mentioning the Jallianwala Bagh massacre by British-led troops in Amritsar (India) in 1919, had written of colonial policy in Africa which "in 1929 mowed down by machine gun fire poor defenceless Nigerian women for peacefully and harmlessly protesting against excessive taxation, the counterpart of India's Amritsar." (Kwame Nkrumah, *Towards Colonial Freedom: Africa in the Struggle against World Imperialism*, Heinemann, London, 1962, p. 35)

As we have seen, both Dr DuBois and the Harlem radical Hubert Harrison had condemned the events leading to or concerning the Jallianwala Bagh incident. Before long, especially with the onset of the sixties, the shooting at Sharpeville in South Africa on March 21, 1960 was to become a synonym for brutal repression. Soweto was yet to come.

With the tide of repression in Africa on the rise, particularly since the fifties as the anti-colonial struggle sharpened, the search for multiple strategies can be understood. In the course of the struggle in India, too, other methods of struggle had not been absent.

Even so, the non-violent strand remained a vital element in African struggles. Congo's Patrice Lumumba, released from prison just in time to attend the Round Table Conference called by the Belgian government in Brussels, observed on the eve of the independence of his country: "We have wrought our freedom by applying the principle of non-violent action in our fight against Colonialism. This we owe to Mahatma Gandhi." (*The Times of India*, January 29, 1960, cited in *Africa Quarterly*, Vol II, No 2, July-September 1962, p. 91)

African leaders like Julius Nyerere spoke a language which in some respects was reminiscent of Gandhi:

"Fellow Africans, be on your guard. The enemy is losing the cold war because he has no argument against our case. His only chance is to provoke violence so that he may use the gun. Don't give him that chance." (Julius K. Nyerere, Sauti Ya Tanu, No 29, May 27, 1958 in *Freedom and Unity : Uhuru na Umoja: A Selection from Writings and Speeches*, 1952-65, Oxford University Press, London, 1967, p. 60)

Another aspect of Gandhi's impact is pointed to by Russell Warren Howe in the Tanzanian context: "Julius Nyerere, the country's leader, was a teacher by profession, and his followers gave him the nickname Mwalimu – 'the learned one'. Greatly influenced by Asian leaders, and especially Gandhi, he sought to impose non-racialism on Tanganyika's revolution. This was a daring piece of wisdom..." (Russell Warren Howe, *Black Africa : From the Colonial Era to Modern Times, Parts 3 and 4,* New Africa Library, London, 1967, p. 294)

On April 7, 1960, in the shadow of the Sharpeville incident, Nkrumah addressed the Positive Action Conference for Peace and Security in Africa. "The beginning of the year 1960", he said, "has seen the climax of ruthless and concerted outrages on the peace-loving people of our continent. The explosion of an atomic device in the Sahara by the French Government and the wanton massacre in the Union of South Africa of our brothers and sisters who were engaged in peaceful demonstrations against humiliating and repulsive laws of the South African Government are two eloquent events in this climax, a climax which is a sign post to the beginning of the end of foreign supremacy and domination in Africa." [Kwame Nkrumah , *Positive Action in Africa,* in James Duffy and Robert A Manners (ed.), *Africa Speaks*, D. Van Nostrand Company, Inc., Princeton, New Jersey, 1961 p. 48]

The atomic tests were a provocation by themselves and more so in the context of the ongoing struggle in Algeria against French rule. Nkrumah saw a still greater need for positive action to resist the emerging challenges. He suggested the adoption of positive action to deal also with the growing atomic dangers, a suggestion that may have some contemporary resonances in the now nuclearised Indian subcontinent:

*"Positive action has already achieved remarkable success in the liberation struggle of our continent and I feel sure that it can further save us from the perils of this atomic arrogance. If the direct action that was carried out by the international protest team were to be repeated on a mass scale, or simultaneously from various parts of Africa, the result could be as powerful and as successful as Gandhi's historic Salt March. We salute Mahatma Gandhi and we remember, in tribute to him, that it was in South Africa that his method of non-violence and non-cooperation was first practiced in the struggle against the vicious race discrimination that still plagues that unhappy country.*

*But now positive action with non-violence, as advocated by us, has found expression in South Africa in the defiance of the oppressive pass laws. This defiance continues in spite of the murder of unarmed men, women, and children by the South African Government. We are sure that the will of the majority will ultimately prevail, for no government can continue to impose its rule in face of the conscious defiance of the overwhelming masses of its people. There is no force, however impregnable, that a united and determined people cannot overcome."* (Ibid. pp 50-51)

As late as the end of the sixties, the West African nationalist pioneer, Dr. Nnamdi Azikiwe wrote in the light of his own experience: "On Gandhi's teachings of satyagraha, history has proved Gandhi right.." (Nnamdi Azikiwe, *My Odyssey: An Autobiography*, Praeger Publishers, New York, 1970, p. 274)

Gandhi's influence in Africa, such as it was, appeared to cut across nations, races, linguistic areas and religions. Among his most ardent students, for example, was Nigeria's Aminu Kano. A devout Muslim, Aminu Kano, according to his biographer, "analysed Gandhi's success in lifting millions of Indians to a high level of dedication and endeavoured to adapt Gandhi's non-violent techniques to Northern Nigeria". (Alan Feinstein, *African Revolutionary: The Life and Times of Nigeria's Aminu Kano*, Davison Publishing House, Devizes, Wiltshire, 1973, pp. 143-144) Kano came, at least according to one source, to be referred to as the "Gandhi of Nigeria" (*Idem*). A progressive Muslim, Aminu Kano took several initiatives for social reform.

A quality that Gandhi came to share with progressive Africa was that of what Desmond Tutu has described as "ubuntu", that is "our sense of connectedness, our sense that my humanity is bound up with your humanity." (Brian Foster, op. cit., p. 25) As Tutu has also put it: "What dehumanises you, inexorably dehumanises me." (Desmond Tutu, *No Future Without Forgiveness*, Rider Books, Random House, London, 1999, p. 35)

Nelson Mandela summed up at the turn of the century:
"Gandhi remained committed to non-violence; I followed the Gandhian strategy for as long as I could, but then there came a point in our struggle when the brute force of the oppressor could no longer be countered through passive resistance alone. We founded Umkhonto we Sizwe and added a military dimension to our struggle. Even then we chose sabotage because it did not involve the loss of life, and it offered the best hope for future race relations." (Nelson Mandela, *The Sacred Warrior: The Liberator of South Africa Looks at the Seminal Work of the Liberator of India, Time*, New York, December 31, 1999)

Mandela stands out as one who was able to forge a positive synthesis between Gandhi's ideas and a restrained resort to force. In this sense he transcended some dismissive attitudes both in India and in Africa towards non-violent struggles.

# INDEX

All personal and place names are sought to be included. No account has been taken of the article "the" in the alphabetical listing of newspapers and articles.

## A



* The alternative spelling 'Abdurrahman' is in conformity with the usage in *The Collected Works of Mahatma Gandhi* (CW) published by the Publications Division, Ministry of Information and Broadcasting, Government of India, New Delhi [1958-1994], i.e., the original or standard edition.

## B

## H



## I

## J

## K



## L



## M

## Z

This book is a richly detailed account of the people and events surrounding Gandhi's experience in Africa and its aftermath. It provides an original narrative of how Gandhi's stance in relation to emancipatory struggles evolved over time, focussing especially on the period since the high noon of his South Africa days. The relationship between Gandhi, Africa and its leaders was mutually productive and symbiotic; a connection which has often been underanalysed.

Through extensive examples and a close reading of documents from the era, the author makes clear the significance of passive or civil resistance as a strategy and traces its contours over Gandhi's lifetime. The resulting book opens up fertile new areas of research and presents us with a holistic picture of the continuing relevance of Gandhi for Africans and Africa for Gandhi.

ANIL NAURIYA is a New Delhi-based lawyer and writes on contemporary history and politics.

**NATIONAL GANDHI MUSEUM**

*in association with*

**GYAN PUBLISHING HOUSE**

**ISBN: 81-87458-13-5** **PRICE Rs. 290/-**